The Business and Economics of Linux® and Open Source

Martin Fink

Prentice Hall PTR
Upper Saddle River, NJ 07458
www.phptr.com

Library of Congress Cataloging-in-Publication Data

Fink, Martin.
    The business and economics of Linux and open source / Martin Fink.
      p. cm.
    Includes bibliographical references and index.
    ISBN 0-13-047677-3
      1. Linux. 2. Business--Computer programs. 3. Open source software. 4. Operating systems (Computers) 5. Computer network resources. I. Title.

HF5548.4.L5 F56 2003
650'0285'54469--dc21

                        2002029260

Editorial/Production Supervision: *Donna Cullen-Dolce*
Executive Editor: *Jill Harry*
Editorial Assistant: *Kate Wolf*
Marketing Manager: *Dan DePasqule*
Manufacturing Buyer: *Maura Zaldivar*
Cover Design Director: *Jerry Votta*
Cover Design: *Nina Scuderi*
Art Director: *Gail Cocker-Bogusz*

Manager, Hewlett-Packard Retail Book Publishing: *Patricia Pekary*

© 2003 by Hewlett-Packard Company
Published by Pearson Education, Inc.
Publishing as Prentice Hall PTR
Upper Saddle River, New Jersey 07458

Prentice Hall books are widely used by corporations and Government agencies for training, marketing, and resale.

For information regarding corporate and government bulk discounts please contact:
Corporate and Government Sales (800) 382-3419 or corpsales@pearsontechgroup.com
Or write: Prentice Hall PTR, Corporate Sales Dept., One Lake Street, Upper Saddle River, NJ 07458.

Company and product names mentioned herein are the trademarks or registered trademarks of their respective owners.

Printed in the United States of America
10   9   8   7   6   5

ISBN 0-13-047677-3

Pearson Education LTD.
Pearson Education Australia PTY, Limited
Pearson Education Singapore, Pte. Ltd.
Pearson Education North Asia Ltd.
Pearson Education Canada, Ltd.
Pearson Educación de Mexico, S.A. de C.V.
Pearson Education—Japan
Pearson Education Malaysia, Pte. Ltd.

To Monique, Cassandra, and Nicholas
For making me so much more than I really am

Contents

Disclaimer and Notices

Acknowledgments

Like many open source projects, I started with the simple notion of solving a problem (in this case, documenting the business side of Linux and open source) without any view of how big the project would be, and how many contributors I would get. I have been delighted with the number of contributors who offered to read and re-read this manuscript under development and offer incredible suggestions to make it much better than it would have been otherwise.

The primary reviewers were Al Stone, Mike Millard, and Katrina Klier. Their comprehensive reviews were enhanced by specific technical and business reviews made by King Ables, Stormy Peters, David Mosberger, Fred Madden, B'Dale Garbee, Doug Mason, Paul Madick, and Jeff Quigley. Some of the information in the chapters on open source processes include content and work by Bruce Perens.

Some reviewers provided input related to their specific areas of expertise or experience. Scott McNeil and Matt Taggart did a great job reviewing the chapter on standards. I had a great deal of legal help from those who make sure I don't really need to go to law school and for this I thank Scott Peterson, Fred Mailman, and especially, Larry Rosen. I offer special thanks to Vern McCrory, who did a great job making sure that my analogies to the pharmaceutical industry were well-grounded in reality, even though I kept them overly simplistic.

I also want to recognize all the people who helped me along the way, including Louise Whissell, Donna Bloechl, Jim Birchfield, Walt Pienkos, Connie Chao, Ralph Hyver, Al Gillen, and Earl Zmijewski.

The executive sponsorship at HP has been equally tremendous with special gratitude to Scott Stallard, Duane Zitzner, and Ed Yang.

Finally, a book like this does not happen without a publisher. I'd like to thank the wonderful people from Prentice Hall, specifically Jill Harry. Additionally, I am grateful for the encouragement of Pat Pekary from HP Books.

Preface

The expression "necessity is the mother of all invention" is so true. I would not have taken on this project if there was another text out there that I could have referenced. Just like every other topic these days, there is an abundance of information on the Internet if you want to do some research. I found no manuscript that consolidates, for a business audience, topics related to Linux and open source in one place. I also believe that some of the paradigm shifts initiated by the open source movement have not been documented for corporate managers, until now.

The Linux and open source movement has instigated "religious wars" between different camps, each presenting extreme but often unrealistic positions. This book is not about any war and does not take on a cause; it is about simple business. This text acknowledges that the Linux and open source phenomenon is real and is rapidly becoming omnipresent within the high-technology industry. However, simple acknowledgment is not enough to deal with the fundamental new business issues created by Linux and open source.

Who This Book Is For

This book is directed primarily at business managers. Some of you will be information technology (IT) managers in any given industry and may be trying to understand what value Linux and open source can deliver to your business. In other words, what is different that would cause you to want to change? Others will be managers developing software for internal use, or for commercial resale. In these cases, you will likely be looking at the open source movement as a way to leverage a huge population of developers, but may struggle to understand the best way to integrate with this community and still return a profit for your investors. This book is from one manager to another and there are two levels of management that can benefit. If you are part of executive management, then this book will give you a guide to help drive your teams to find the right answers and help you ask the right questions when your teams make new proposals related to Linux and open source. If you are in the middle management ranks, this book should help you make sure that your plans and proposals to senior management are complete and address the new business paradigms of Linux and open source.

This book is not for developers. It does not navigate through any code modules for any software in Linux or any other open source project. There may be cases where uninitiated developers may be looking for a big-picture view of the Linux and open source communities. In these cases, this book will add value, at least in parts.

For the past few years, I have been working every day in this wonderful new way of doing business. It is always a challenge to take on a job where concepts are different and some of the fundamental rules change. It is natural for most people to reject these changes and do everything possible to maintain the status quo. I continue to deal with this resistance every day. While the business concepts associated with Linux and open source are still very new, corporate managers are rapidly discovering that they can no longer ignore what is happening. The wonderful thing about a market economy is that it requires new business concepts such as Linux and open source to prove themselves, and once proven, those who ignore them, invariably lose. Competitors who take notice and aggressively take advantage of new opportunities begin to take business from those who reject change. However, those who move too quickly to every fad that comes around waste resources and eventually either disappear or realign to an accepted business reality. There are those who believe that Linux and open source are still a passing fad, and some who even hope it will go away soon. The Linux operating system is now more than 10 years old.

The open source movement, which started with the free software movement, is approaching 20 years of existence. It should be apparent that it is not going away, and that your business needs to deal with new realities.

HOW THIS BOOK IS ORGANIZED

Part 1 of the book is an initiation into the world of Linux and open source. Chapter 1 starts by examining the fundamental business reasons why this new movement is good for business and how it delivers value. It also establishes a core understanding of terminology and significant players so that you can follow the rest of the book. Chapter 2 digs deep into the Linux kernel. While the kernel may seem a deeply technical topic for business, in this new world, it is a core requirement to understand how the components fit together. The next chapter outlines the Open Source Definition. Since open source is at the core of what makes Linux work, understanding open source licenses is also a required component of basic training. Part 1 ends with a broad look at a number of communities and organizations you will need to be familiar with as you integrate your company with this movement.

Part 2 looks at the operational side of Linux. It starts with a look at Linux distributions to help you internalize how the Linux kernel integrates with all the pieces that constitute an operating system. Next, you will be taken through a detailed analysis of measuring IT costs with an open source mindset. We will also look at how key standards affect the cost picture and which ones will be important to the future success of Linux. Finally, we will take a look at operations from deployment, migration, and coexistence, to support and training.

The last part of this book explores in great detail the open source effect on the corporations and businesses developing commercial software. This is where the fundamental new business paradigms are examined. We will start by looking at how the open source community is structured, some of its cultural elements, and how it compares to a corporate structure. We will also examine the open source effect on the value delivered over time. This will prepare you for the following discussion, which is a detailed examination of open source business models and how to make money. The last two chapters examine in great detail the process of integrating open source within your company and the people management effects of working with this new community of developers.

Many of the concepts presented, especially in Part 3, will be very new to a business audience. Hopefully the information will give you enough guidance to manage open source projects within your company and help you build synergistic relationships with the great communities of developers out there.

As you being to understand how open source works and what it really is, I encourage you to look at this book as an open source project. I am but the maintainer, and I hope that any of you will become contributors. I present to you an imperfect project and hope you will share your genius, much as those who contributed to the review process, to evolve it into a great one.

Martin Fink
Summer 2002

Groundwork

Welcome to the world of Linux and open source. This book assumes that you have a technology background, but does not assume prior knowledge of Linux and open source. Part 1 lays a foundation of basic knowledge that you need to navigate and understand an open source operating system, development model, and licensing process.

Chapter 1 will give you the business basics of why you need to care about Linux and open source. Chapter 2 will detail the core of the Linux kernel. Chapter 3 will walk you through the Open Source Definition and its associated licenses. Finally, Chapter 4 will give a view of just how big the open source movement really is.

The Business of Linux and Open Source

*L*inux and open source present many new technologies, ideas, concepts, and paradigms. Linux is a major new operating system that was developed using open source methodologies. To delve into what Linux is and how open source development can affect your enterprise, a crash course in some of these new concepts is required. The goals for this chapter are for you to understand:

- Where Linux is used and how it is growing
- Terminology that will be useful in understanding the book
- The key business benefits of Linux and open source
- Major inhibitors limiting the growth of Linux
- Major players in the open source community

This chapter explains why Linux and open source are important to your business and gives you the base foundation that will enable you to progress through the book.

Linux Adoption

Normally we look at charts that show the revenue that a product or service is expected to generate in the marketplace. That picture cannot be accurate for Linux as it is impossible to accurately count the actual number of copies of Linux in use. This is very difficult to do for Linux because

Linux is open source. Yes, it is possible to purchase copies of Linux. But, most often, companies will purchase one copy, customize it, and reuse the customized copy throughout the enterprise. Linux can also be downloaded from numerous places for free, built from scratch, included with books, and bundled with any number of products. Some users also configure their systems in a dual-boot configuration to allow the use of multiple different operating systems on the same computer. This makes the task of counting the actual number of copies of Linux in use very difficult, although many industry analysts, such as what IDC published and represented in Figure 1–1, are attempting approximations. Figure 1–1 enumerates the number of copies (both free and purchased) of Linux operating environments in use.

As I mentioned, since Linux itself can be obtained for free, the market revenue of the Linux operating system itself tends to be meaningless. But, having an approximate view of the copies in use gives you a leading indicator of what associated product revenues, such as clients, software, storage, and others, will be. This chart gives you a view of how fast Linux has been growing and that its growth is not stopping anytime soon. Notice that you must consider free as well as purchased copies. You should logically infer from this that companies in many technology segments will shift future product investments to Linux to take advantage of this growth.

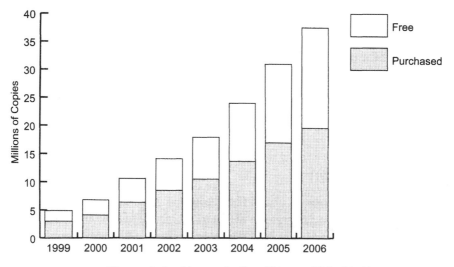

Figure 1–1   Linux adoption (Source: IDC, 2002).

Crash Course in Linux and Open Source Lingo

By the time you finish this book, you will have a solid understanding of how Linux and open source work and apply to your business. However, an early crash course on some key terminology will help us get through some of the early parts of this book. This set of explanations is only meant to give you enough understanding to make it through the book. Most of these concepts will be explained in detail as the book progresses.

- **Kernel**—The kernel is the heart of the operating system that manages the key resources (such as memory, processes, etc.) on your system. Linux is in fact a kernel, not an operating system.
- **GNU**—This is a recursive acronym for **G**NU's, **N**ot **U**NIX. As you can see the first letter of the acronym is the acronym itself. Whereas Linux is the kernel of the operating system, the GNU system represents many of the other parts (compilers, tools, editors, etc.) needed to have a useful system. Purists contend that referring to Linux as the operating system is erroneous and it should be referred to as the GNU/Linux system, an important distinction to keep in mind as you discuss Linux opportunities in your company.
- **Distribution**—Most companies that deploy or develop applications for Linux will usually do this by acquiring a distribution. Some of the more common Linux distributions are Red Hat, SuSE, Debian, Mandrake, Connectiva, and Red Flag. Distribution vendors combine the Linux kernel, many parts of the GNU system, other open source components, and enhancements of their own to distribute the whole as an integrated and tested system. In many instances, distributions are targeted at specific sectors or specific geographies of the market.
- **Package**—The individual components installed on a Linux system are distributed as packages. Generically, a package refers to any collection of files distributed together to serve a specific purpose. Since many packages can share the same set of files, complex interdependencies are managed by installation and deployment tools.
- **Free software**—Free is meant to signify freedom, as in free speech, and not to characterize "without cost." Free software originated with the Free Software Foundation under the premise that all software should be shared and everyone should have equal access to source code, or the blueprints of the system.

- **Open source**—This term will generally be used in two contexts: first, as the marketing phrase for free software; and second, as a development methodology that I will cover in great detail in Part 3. While the leaders of the free software movement tend to object to the association with open source, the term was coined to overcome the common misconception that free software implied software without cost. Open source is *not* a license. It provides a common set of specifications to which licenses must adhere to be considered open source.
- **Community**—Any collection of software developers working collaboratively on a software project. A community can represent students, hobbyists, corporate developers, competitors, and customers, among many others.
- **Maintainer**—The individual, committee, board of directors, or foundation that accepts or rejects code changes into an open source project. You can also think of the maintainer as the project manager. Probably the most well-known maintainer is Linus Torvalds (the creator of the Linux kernel).
- **GPL**—This stands for the GNU general public license. The GPL will be covered in depth in Chapter 3. For now, understanding that the GPL is the most frequently used open source license will suffice. The GPL is the license that governs the Linux kernel. The GPL requires that any modifications to the source base be returned to the community at large.

This list of terms should be enough to get you going. As you read through the book, refer back to these to make sure you have a solid grasp of these key terms. By the time you finish the book, most of these should be very familiar to you.

Linux Workloads

Figure 1–2 demonstrates the key places where Linux is being used and how usage is expanding over time. In the server realm, Linux is strongest at the edge of the network. This is largely due to the powerful combination created by the Linux operating system and Apache Web Server. These appliance-like devices draw on the strength of Linux as a network operating system.

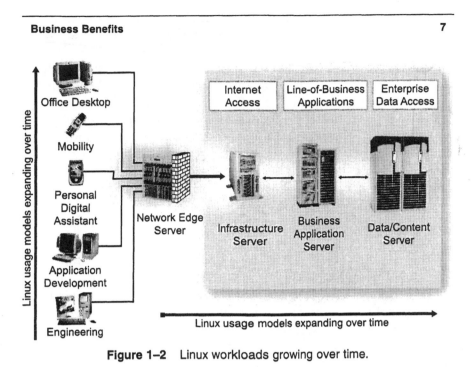

Figure 1–2 Linux workloads growing over time.

As Linux matures, it will gradually see its application workloads evolve to the infrastructure and application server tiers. The great debate is how long this evolution will take and how far Linux will push into the enterprise data center. On the client side, Linux, with its heritage of being a UNIX-like operating system, has naturally gained popularity with engineering workstations and application development systems. Linux has also started to penetrate the embedded device arena. The great debate here is whether or not Linux will become a viable operating system for the general office desktop. While these are general adoption trends, there are pockets of adoption already scattered in virtually all areas of the computing spectrum.

Business Benefits

Linux has rapidly evolved from a niche and hobbyist toy to a credible environment in use at many businesses. Much of Linux's initial transition into the business world was as a result of the Internet boom. Service providers saw Linux as a way to deploy systems using commodity components and not have any costs associated with licensing either the operating system or key open source applications such as the Apache Web Server and other programs that are essential to the Internet and that run well under Linux. Service providers tend to have highly technical personnel, thereby rendering vendor support a controllable issue. Mainstream businesses are now seeing that Linux is maturing as a credible alternative to other operating environments from the cost, resource, and control perspectives. Here are some of the key business benefits of Linux:

Cost

The fact that Linux can be freely copied, subject to reasonable license terms, without payment of royalties is clearly viewed by many as one of the main business advantages of Linux. Although it is possible for you to deploy Linux without paying license fees, this does not mean that Linux, or any operating system, is "free" in the sense that there are no costs associated with its installation, maintenance, support, and training. In Chapter 6, we will take a detailed look at some of the new and different cost considerations associated with Linux (and many other open source software).

Availability of Trained Resources

Linux is now more than 10 years old and so trained resources are available. The cost advantages of Linux have enticed many education and research institutions such as the University of Waterloo in Ontario, Canada, the University of Illinois at Urbana-Champaign/NCSA (National Center for Super Computing Applications), and many others to deploy Linux aggressively. This has now been happening for a few years. For example, the Groupe ESIEE in France, a center for advanced scientific and technical education, has been using Linux for three years because Linux is open source. They state their motivation very simply: ESIEE develops for the community, and the community develops for ESIEE. It is a simple return on investment for the center. The University of New South Wales converted all of their UNIX-based teaching labs to Linux in one year. The result is that many, many new graduates are fully trained and well-versed in the Linux operating system, even more so than in most flavors of UNIX.

It also follows that the newest generations of developers are all trained and have built their expertise on Linux and its associated application programming interfaces (APIs). Many of the most popular companion open source applications, such as the Apache Web Server, are also very familiar to this new generation.

Figure 1–3 shows the key Linux stakeholders that represent core competence in the Linux movement and resources you can draw on.

As your enterprise grows and you need more talented personnel to run your network infrastructure, application servers, and data center, Linux-capable talent will be one of the most readily available resources.

Support

One of the raging debates about Linux is the issue of where support comes from. One side of the debate argues that since Linux is maintained and enhanced by a community of loosely coupled developers, the ability to get guaranteed support is questionable. The other side of the debate argues that since the code is available to all, anyone can provide support and that self-support now becomes a lower cost and more viable option. Which side of the debate you take will depend largely on the type of information technology (IT) organization you have built and your previous experiences with various vendors. The benefit to you is that you have the choice of which support model to implement and anyone can provide support. Chapter 8 will go into the details of support options and the implications of the choices you make.

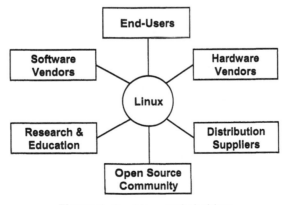

Figure 1–3   Linux stakeholders.

Control and Vendor Independence

The Intel x86 architecture (also known as IA-32) brought commodity economics to the personal computer (PC). In many ways, Linux does the same thing for the operating system. Prior to Linux, your choice was primarily a proprietary operating system on proprietary hardware, or a proprietary operating system on commodity hardware. While there are other open source operating systems such as BSD, Linux is the first viable combination of a commodity operating system on commodity hardware (Linux is also available on a wide range of proprietary and embedded architectures). As you will discover later, the licensing model used by Linux is what has differentiated it from BSD and created a single operating system developed by many. With more and more independent software vendors (ISVs) making their applications available on Linux, IT managers can now deploy solutions on the hardware and operating environment that is the most cost-effective and delivers the highest return.

Enterprises that have deployed commodity hardware on the Intel IA-32 architecture have seen the many benefits of commodity economics. Companies are no longer tied to one vendor and the switching costs are very low. Companies also have the choice to mix and match hardware and peripherals since a large ecosystem develops around commodity products. Most, if not all, of these same advantages, which boil down to choice and control, are available with Linux. If one Linux operating system vendor does not provide the level of service or quality your company needs, then switch. If the support does not measure up, find someone else or do it yourself. The do-it-yourself option is one that is much more viable with open source software than with commodity hardware. With commodity hardware, you still need to work with one hardware vendor for the features or defect repairs you need. With software, you can implement changes on your own or seek the help of professionals to do it on your behalf.

Software Development

Linux has become the primary platform for Fluent's development team. Fluent is a leading vendor of computer-aided engineering (CAE) software solutions. Linux gives Fluent's developers an extremely fast and stable platform with a wealth of freeware tools. In addition, developers have complete access to all Windows applications via VMware, an Intel chip emulator that runs under Linux. This gives them access to both UNIX and Windows environments from a single machine.

By almost any measure, Windows with Visual Studio continues to grab the lion's share of the software development market. But, if you segment out the UNIX market, the software development activity is rapidly shifting to Linux. A significant part of this phenomenon is driven by the education and research market mentioned earlier.

Upgrades

Today, Linux is considered to be rock-solid for many application workloads. Every year, companies spend millions of dollars upgrading applications or environments that work just fine. Much of the motivation for the upgrades is due to hardware and licensing requirements by various vendors. With Linux, you are in control. You have the option to consider the costs of self-support, buying support, or doing upgrades and making the best set of tradeoffs for your business. It is not uncommon for users to skip many upgrade opportunities until there is a compelling business benefit and a return for the costs and risks of upgrading an environment. One of the beauties of open source is that you decide when to do this, not the vendor. Hardware is also not necessarily obsolete simply because you upgrade your software. Many developers in the community are making very productive use of systems as much as 10 years old, which are considered obsolete by most others.

It is well understood by most corporations that change implies risks and opportunities, both of which need to be measured and qualified just as any other operational activity within the corporation. If you deploy an environment, no license in the Linux and open source world will compel you to change, downgrade, or upgrade that environment. It is also always possible for you to obtain and use old versions of software. You are in complete control of your environment; therefore, you control the success/failure of your network, and ultimately, your business.

Inhibitors to Linux Growth

Linux is not a panacea to solve all the woes of the average IT department. It is clearly a new opportunity to lower costs, maintain or expand functionality, and partner with a huge community of developers that would be too expensive for anyone to hire. Let's explore some of the more significant inhibitors holding Linux back. As with most things in the high-tech world, there is a large contingent working diligently to eliminate any inhibitors to Linux's growth. Time will eliminate many of the inhibitors listed here.

Application Availability

Linux owes much of its success to one killer open source application: the Apache Web Server. According to the Netcraft Web server survey (*www.netcraft.com*), at the end of 2001, the Apache Web Server was being used by more than 50% of sites on the Internet. The combination of Linux and Apache creates a low-cost, high-performance, easily deployed environment for almost any service provider or IT department.

Beyond Apache, many applications have been developed by research and educational communities, or have been developed in-house by companies on the leading edge.

The classic chicken-and-egg conundrum occurs with any environment, and Linux is no different. While many companies wait for applications to be available before they deploy Linux in their environment, ISVs wait for customers to deploy Linux before they make their applications available.

This chicken-and-egg conundrum is gradually breaking down, however. Part of the breakdown is attributed to the normal maturation of Linux. Also, mainstream application vendors are seeing part of their business being eroded by open source alternatives. One of the first and most significant of these breakdowns was the effect of Apache on the Netscape Web server family.

Another factor driving the change is one already mentioned: the development environment. ISVs have had to maintain multiple development environments for each of their UNIX platforms. Many are shifting to Linux as their core development environment and using it as the base port for all other platforms. In fact, in conversations with ISVs, many of them were surprised to find that a significant portion of their engineers were already using Linux both at work and at home. Some of them expected huge efforts to port to Linux, only to discover that it was already done (or at least, large parts were finished).

Large hardware and software companies are fully supporting Linux. Now that BEA, Dell, Hewlett-Packard (HP), International Business Machines (IBM), Oracle, SAP, and many others are making products available on Linux, the ecosystems around each of these (and many other) companies are also planning to support their products and services on Linux. The snowball is well on its way down the mountain and steadily gaining momentum.

Of course, paying customers have the final say. As more and more companies request, and even demand Linux, vendors will have no choice but to respond.

Maturity

Maturity is a relative term. But, 10 years is actually very young for an operating system, especially when compared to UNIX, which has a heritage that goes back to the 1960s. Linux has a solid and proven track record in the Internet infrastructure. As we saw from Figure 1–2, it is also starting to make inroads in the application server tier. Many of the critical infrastructure applications (databases, application servers, etc.) needed for core business applications are now becoming available.

Another area of maturity can be classified as "enterprise-readiness." IT managers count on a broad range of tools and capabilities to manage large environments. However, many of the system management, administration, deployment, and update tools that most IT managers take for granted are either not available or very early in their stages of development. Hardware vendors, software vendors, and the open source community at large are working diligently to fill these gaps. This obstacle will be overcome faster as companies put their own engineers to work part-time or full-time on improving this state of Linux. By opting to use this potential control point, companies of any size can influence the direction and development speed of Linux—a luxury not available to many in the past with other operating systems.

Many software vendors are also looking for additional features in the Linux kernel to be able to tune the performance, availability, and scalability of their applications. Today, many of them make compromises to overcome some of these limitations. Again, the open source community provides a proactive forum to solve these limitations in ways not tied to company budgets, roadmaps, financials, or legal constraints.

Scalability

Vertical scalability allows Linux to scale its performance by adding processors within the same system. Horizontal scalability increases scale by distributing tasks among many systems. Scalability is a relative characteristic. For many, many applications, Linux scales very well. With the release of the Linux 2.4 kernel, multi-processor scalability to 16 processors is usually possible, provided the application can take advantage of it. Today's UNIX systems will often scale to 128 processors and beyond.

However, scalability can take many other forms. Many of those who need scalability beyond what Linux can deliver and also want the cost advantages have turned to clusters to solve their performance needs. Horizontal scalability, or combining a large number of low-cost systems and making them work in tandem, has been and continues to be one of the great strengths of Linux. However, applications are usually developed and tuned to scale well in either multiprocessor or clustered environments. Rarely will applications be optimized to scale well in both configurations. Linux also has many opportunities to improve scalability in input/output (I/O) capabilities, availability, deployment, and management.

The scalability of the Linux kernel continues to be an area of debate. The changes to the kernel involve difficult tradeoffs between complexity and capability. Linus Torvalds, the creator of the Linux kernel (discussed in detail in the next chapter), has tended to err on the side of keeping the kernel small, reducing complexity, and optimizing for smaller systems. This may make it more difficult to find ways to vertically scale the kernel.

Business Risk

Linux (and most open source software) presents a new class of business risks, usually involving the management of intellectual property. Implementing any new technology within an enterprise involves risk that needs to be managed. Linux and open source are no different. Business processes that may not have existed before must be established. Many companies are discovering, however, that managing these risks responsibly are well worth the economic returns that Linux brings. Part 3 of this book will examine, in significant detail, many of the risks associated with open source and how to manage them. In fact, open source opens a wealth of new opportunities to increase productivity and refocus your energy to the core value you bring to your customers.

Who's Who in Open Source?

The community is a collection of individuals around the world working on open source projects. Some do this work as part of their normal duties assigned by their employers; others do it in their spare time because they love the work. Some are driven by simple ego, some by their belief in open source, and others by their desire for more creative answers to their problems. Many of these developers are part of the education and research community. Figure 1–4 shows a basic timeline of significant events in the life of Linux and open source.

In Part 3 of this book, we will cover the reasons why companies encourage and sponsor their employees to work on open source projects.

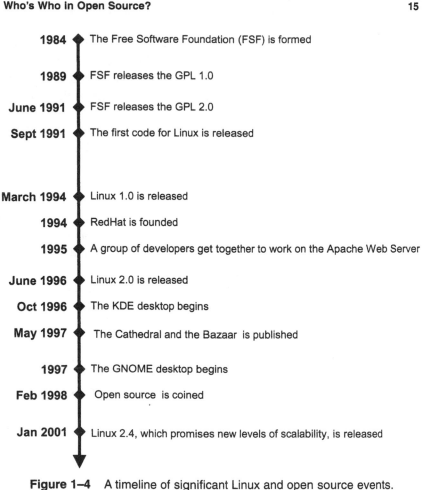

1984 ◆ The Free Software Foundation (FSF) is formed

1989 ◆ FSF releases the GPL 1.0

June 1991 ◆ FSF releases the GPL 2.0

Sept 1991 ◆ The first code for Linux is released

March 1994 ◆ Linux 1.0 is released

1994 ◆ RedHat is founded

1995 ◆ A group of developers get together to work on the Apache Web Server

June 1996 ◆ Linux 2.0 is released

Oct 1996 ◆ The KDE desktop begins

May 1997 ◆ The Cathedral and the Bazaar is published

1997 ◆ The GNOME desktop begins

Feb 1998 ◆ Open source is coined

Jan 2001 ◆ Linux 2.4, which promises new levels of scalability, is released

Figure 1–4   A timeline of significant Linux and open source events.

For now, there are a few key names and a few significant events that are useful to know and understand their role and impact within the community.

I can't list everyone who has an important role, and I am sure I will bruise a few egos by not including them in this list. The fact is that there are many I have not listed here who play critical roles in many communities. You will learn later that open source is largely a game of influence and relationships. Once you understand the communities that are important to your business, you will be well-served to invest time and energy in building relationships with the leaders and participants of that community.

- **Linus Torvalds**—Probably the most known personality in the Linux and open source world, Linus is the creator and maintainer of the Linux kernel. He maintains the platform-independent parts of the kernel, and the components of the core kernel that are specific to the Intel IA-32 architecture. Ports of Linux to other architectures are each maintained by separate groups and individuals.
- **Alan Cox**—Until the fall of 2001, Alan was considered Linus' top lieutenant. As you will learn in Chapter 2, Linus maintained the Linux kernel currently in development, while Alan maintained the currently released kernel. As is typical within the community, when Alan decided he wanted to work on other things, he chose a successor to take on his present task. Although Alan is not longer the maintainer of the released Linux kernel, he still commands tremendous influence and respect within the community.
- **Marcelo Tosatti**—Linus and Alan transferred the maintenance torch of the stable Linux kernel (the kernel considered to be in production) to Marcelo. Since Linus must work closely with this individual, he obviously needed to be part of the selection process. Marcelo is a very capable kernel developer who has demonstrated considerable aptitude at working with the community of kernel developers.
- **Dave Miller**—If you submit changes to the networking stacks in the Linux kernel, David is the developer who will likely check your submission and decide if it should be accepted. Think of David as the keeper of Linux networking.
- **Richard Stallman**—The founder of the FSF. Richard is also the creator of the GNU GPL. Richard continues to play an influential role in the free software movement. Many will seek his guidance when clarity is needed with certain areas of the GPL.
- **Bruce Perens**—As the project leader for the Debian project (we will cover Debian in depth later), Bruce authored a "Social Contract" to instill a standard code of conduct when working with free software on the project. When the term "open source" was coined, this "Social Contract" became the Open Source Definition (OSD). Bruce is therefore known as the primary author of the OSD. Chapter 3 outlines this definition in detail.
- **Eric Raymond**—Known as an anthropologist and thought leader within the open source community, Eric is now well-known for his groundbreaking paper, "The Cathedral and the Bazaar," which outlined the open source development process, why it works, and how it can be replicated. Part 3 of this book extends Eric's work to the commercial enterprise.

- **Larry Augustin**—Larry is the CEO of VA Software Corporation. VA Software was originally incorporated as VA Linux Systems. Larry was one of the first to recognize the value of Linux and open source. He created the first hardware company dedicated to supporting Linux. As mainstream hardware vendors such as Dell, IBM, HP, and others began to support Linux, Larry changed his business model to sell software that supports the open source collaborative development process within corporations.
- **Tim O'Reilly**—As the President of O'Reilly Books, Tim continues to have a tremendous influence on the open source movement. The O'Reilly network encompasses key open source technologies such as Perl and others in wide use throughout the Internet. Tim provides a voice for the community by publishing many of their ideas.
- **Brian Behlendorf**—Brian is the co-founder of the Apache Software Foundation. Since Apache has been the open source killer application, Brian has had an influential role not only within the Apache movement, but also the community at large.
- **Michael Tiemann**—Michael founded Cygnus Solutions, the first commercial company based on an open source business model. Cygnus provided the infrastructure for a key component of Linux: compilers. Cygnus pioneered many of the business models based on providing support, services, and other enhancements to free software. Cygnus was acquired by Red Hat in 2000.
- **Bob Young**—Bob is credited with the success of today's most popular Linux distribution, Red Hat. Bob used his marketing savvy to create a powerful brand around the Linux operating system, and in many ways, brought Linux to the masses. Today, Bob is on the board of directors of Red Hat and speaks frequently at Linux and open source events.
- **Jeremy Allison**—Jeremy is the leader of the SAMBA project. As you will discover, SAMBA is key interoperability technology used between the UNIX/Linux and Windows worlds. SAMBA is core technology that is included with most Linux distributions.
- **Miguel de Icaza**—Miguel is a founder and currently CTO of Ximian (formerly Helix Code) Corporation. Miguel led the development of the GNOME desktop environment for many years. Today, Miguel is leading another ground breaking open source project called Mono (Spanish for monkey, the company's mascot). Mono is an open source implementation of a subset of the Microsoft .NET framework.

Summary

You now have a core foundation of knowledge we can build on. You also see that Linux brings many opportunities for you to reduce your IT costs, but that open source presents new business risks that must be managed. With a core understanding of key terms and knowing the major players, we can now start to explore the specifics of how you can take advantage of these benefits and manage the risks within your enterprise.

The rest of Part 1 will expand your understanding of the Linux operating system, and go into the details of open source and the associated licenses. Part 1 ends with an overview of the more significant open source communities that you will likely encounter and need to work with. Part 2 will take a look at the operational side of Linux, encouraging you to consider what you need to deploy in your enterprise, along with providing information about the support, migration, and cost implications of Linux. Part 3 will dig into managing the business risks and opportunities of open source. It will outline not only how to work with open source projects, but also how to implement the development methodology in your environment.

Linux—Heart of the Operating System

"*L*inux" usually refers to the whole operating system. For the most part, thinking of Linux that way is fine. However, Linux is actually a small part of an overall working system. Technically, Linux is only the kernel, the core foundation that keeps an overall system functioning properly. There are many other parts that complete the operating system. A significant number of tools usually delivered as part of the Linux operating system are collectively called the GNU system. Richard Stallman frequently asserts that referring to Linux as the operating system is erroneous, and that the total system should be called the GNU/Linux system. However, there are other components such as the X11 windowing system, desktop interfaces, file-sharing interoperability tools, and many others that are also usually delivered with Linux, so the name GNU/Linux is also not entirely accurate. Formally, Linux is a registered trademark for "computer operating system software to facilitate computer use and operation." Linus Torvalds owns the Linux trademark.

Choosing to deploy Linux in your enterprise requires a clear understanding of the components of Linux. Therefore, the goals for this chapter are to understand:

- A simple view of an operating system
- The Linux kernel and how it compares to other types of kernels
- How the Linux kernel is developed and updated, as well as its versioning system

- How kernel functionality is extended through the use of modules and patches
- Fragmentation (or forking) considerations with Linux
- The multiplatform aspects of Linux
- The most significant uses of Linux

This chapter explores some sophisticated technical concepts. Operating system kernels are by their very nature a difficult topic. The goal is to gain some familiarity with these advanced topics to understand how they impact IT decisions in key areas of deployment, migration, and development projects. Also, many IT managers fear a repeat of the old "UNIX wars" that caused fragmentation and resulted in the many different UNIX variants in the marketplace today. Increasing your understanding of Linux and its structure will help you will make sure you have the facts you will need to make your IT decisions and help allay any lingering "UNIX war" fears. Put on your propeller hat and prepare to find out why Linux is different.

In Chapter 5, we will examine Linux distributions. Whereas Linux is the kernel, distributions combine the Linux kernel with the GNU system and many of the other parts needed to have a functioning system. In many cases, a distribution will contain all the functionality you need for a useful system. In other cases, you will procure add-on applications.

The Operating System

There is no fully accepted standard of what an operating system should include, since the component parts that are included in any system have usually evolved substantially over time. In the mid to late 1980s, when networking was still new, many companies sold core networking stacks (such as TCP/IP) as add-ons to popular operating systems. As networking evolved to be a core requirement of virtually all applications on a system, the network stacks became part of the base for most operating systems.

The debate of what constitutes an operating system continues to rage on as some vendors include certain components and others don't. Nevertheless, in a general way, most vendors consider Figure 2–1 to be a simplified view of the components of an operating system. The Linux operating system includes all of these components.

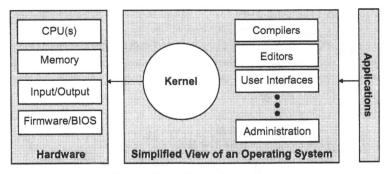

Figure 2–1 Operating system.

As you can see, the operating system is the link between the applications you need to run your business and the resources (the hardware components) available to you. The more applications and users utilizing the system, the more work the operating system needs to do. Consumer operating systems include many applications to enhance the end-user experience (music players, image manipulators, etc.). Operating systems focused on the corporate world support applications focused at managing many users, and a primary objective is to control computer resources at minimal cost.

Resource utilization in Linux can be thought of in three dimensions: (1) management, (2) administration, and (3) control.

From an operating system perspective, *resource management* provides a global view of computer resources available and how they are deployed and used. For instance, if you run an airline, you make sure that you have deployed your aircraft for optimal revenue based on the routes that return the most profit. Similarly, in Linux, resource management components help manage your computer hardware components in a coherent way.

Once you have deployed your computer resources, *resource administration* tools in Linux help you configure these available resources in the most efficient manner possible. Your airline equivalent would be making sure you have set up your aircraft with the right amount of fuel, food for passengers, and the proper crew.

Resource control also falls under the purview of the Linux operating system kernel. The kernel controls available resources based on its design and configuration, just as your aircraft will travel as high and as fast as its design specifications allow.

The Linux Kernel

Technically speaking, Linux is the kernel of the operating system. Figure 2–2 outlines the key components of a kernel. A simple way to think of a kernel is to think of the engine in an aircraft. While the engine provides the power for the aircraft, pilots do not interact directly with the engine. The kernel is the power in your operating system that the users of the computer never directly see. In real terms, the kernel is one large application that controls your system. This application has complete control and authority over all the resources (disks, memory, CPU, etc.) on your system. It is the job of the kernel to manage and respond to all of the incoming requests (from applications and users) for system resources. How efficiently the kernel does this depends on its overall design and configuration.

Kernel Design

Linux is a monolithic kernel. As Figure 2–2 depicts, all of the kernel components are contained as one special, large application running on the system. The kernel is a special type of application, with special privileges, whose job is to control your system. The term "application" should not be confused with applications you use to run your day-to-day business. Any information about the state of the kernel is available to all components of the kernel.

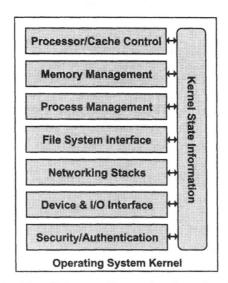

Figure 2–2   Monolithic operating system kernel and functions.

Another type of kernel used in modern operating systems is the micro-kernel. Micro-kernels break apart most of the key control functions. Rather than state information being available to all functions, messages are passed from one function to another. Figure 2–3 demonstrates a simple micro-kernel architecture.

Proponents of micro-kernels argue that they increase modularity, portability, and performance. Others, such as Linus Torvalds, argue that the message passing required between each of the control modules increases complexity and makes the kernel more prone to obscure defects.

Of historical interest is the fact that Richard Stallman was developing a kernel for his GNU system that was based on a micro-kernel architecture, the GNU Hurd kernel. Richard admits that the development and debugging complexity associated with the GNU Hurd slowed development considerably. Linus Torvald's monolithic kernel was developed far more rapidly and became available to support the GNU system well before the GNU Hurd was ready.

Linux Kernel Modules

One of the key advances of the 2.0 version of the Linux kernel was its use of modules. Prior to this, any new functionality or capability added to the kernel had to be compiled into the kernel and the system restarted

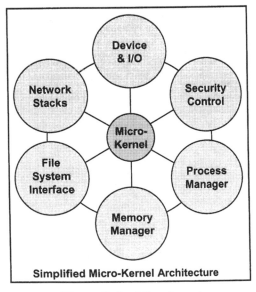

Figure 2–3   Micro-kernel.

to make it available. Modules provide a mechanism to extend the functionality of the Linux kernel while the system is running.

The most common way in which modules are used is via "device drivers." A device driver is the software link between the operating system and a device. In our aircraft analogy, think of device drivers as throttle, navigation, and other mechanisms that the pilot uses to control the plane. Pilots use these controls without worrying about the specifics of the engine itself. Device drivers require access to information about the current state of the kernel. Device drivers also need to be controlled by other kernel components.

Most device drivers are written by individual members of a large and disparate open source development community. Also, it is almost impossible to determine at the time a kernel is built all of the different possible device and system configurations that will be needed by an end-user. Without modules, every possible device driver would need to be compiled into the kernel. This would significantly increase the size (or memory footprint) of the kernel, potentially making the system less efficient.

Since Linux version 2.0, modules are extensions that can be bolted into, and unbolted from, the operating system at almost any time. Figure 2–4 shows how kernel modules fit into Linux.

In the open source paradigm, everyone has the ability to change or extend the Linux kernel's functionality through the use of modules.

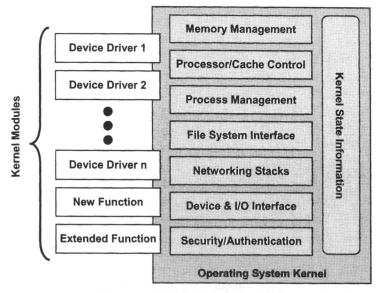

Figure 2–4   Linux kernel modules.

Linux Kernel Patches

Just as modules provide a mechanism to add new functionality to the Linux kernel, patches provide a way to extend or change kernel functionality without compromising the integrity of the Linux kernel as released by Linus Torvalds. Patches are often thought of as a mechanism to repair defects. With Linux, patches are also used to change or add functionality to the kernel. Again using the aircraft analogy, where throttle and navigation controls were the device drivers, patches will in some cases represent repairs to the engine and in others will be ways to implement new functions, such as adding special cooling capabilities to your engine.

As you deploy Linux in your enterprise or build new applications to work on Linux, you will want to take careful note of your dependencies, not just on a kernel version, but also on any patches and modules that may need to be installed.

Kernel Fragmentation (or Forking)

One of the biggest concerns newcomers have when considering Linux is the notion of fragmentation. Kernel fragmentation is also called "forking the kernel." In any case, it refers to a proliferation of various different kernel implementations.

The root of this concern stems from the history of the UNIX wars. UNIX originally had the promise of being one system with one common set of programming interfaces. Porting your application from one UNIX system to another was supposed to be a simple matter of recompiling for the new target system. However, UNIX vendors needed to differentiate their offerings. So, each vendor would extend and add new functionality to the operating system, and in many cases, the functionality was implemented in radically different ways. The end result was that although all UNIX systems shared a common heritage and functioned in much the same way, each vendor's UNIX was different enough to force significant application porting efforts when moving from one version to another. These differences also created "lock-ins" that increased your costs when you switched from a vendor who was not delivering value to your satisfaction.

ISVs face the brunt of the work caused by each of these disparate UNIX flavors. The ISVs need to balance the costs of porting and supporting each new computer platform, while achieving the broadest possible market. Each supported platform requires extensive tuning, verification, and support. Forks of the kernel dramatically increase costs for ISVs and their customers.

When corporations and ISVs are initiated to Linux and hear the names of many Linux commercial distributors (such as Red Hat, SuSE, Turbolinux, Mandrake, and others), they sometimes fear a repeat of the UNIX wars. *However, all Linux distributions share a common Linux kernel, and this is what makes Linux different*. The common Linux kernel helps eliminate significant porting/support cost concerns, allowing for simplified pricing and market delivery of ISV products compared with what ISVs have faced in the past with UNIX.

While everyone operates under the concept of a common kernel, patches and other features can create differences between distribution vendors. Chapter 7 will walk you through the relevant standards that are compensating for these differences.

The Linux kernel is open source. The fact that the kernel is open source removes the ability and incentive for vendors to differentiate at such a low level in the value chain. A view into this value chain and where differentiation is possible will be covered in Chapter 5 when Linux distributions are covered in detail. The beauty of this open source paradigm is that vendors are now highly motivated to cooperate and share with the community at large, and among each other, to extend the functionality of the system to meet higher level goals. Software vendors reduce their development costs while focusing on higher value for customers. ISVs can count on one common base for development and deployment of their applications. Corporations can finally benefit from a common system across vendors and focus on the needs of their business rather than the individual low-level functionality of each vendor's operating environment.

While the open source nature of Linux makes fragmentation high unlikely, corporations and ISVs do need to manage some complexities in the Linux environment. The kernel has evolved, just as any other system, and there are now multiple versions available. ISVs, freelance developers, and other solution vendors may create patches that force dependencies to be managed. Thus, there is a large selection of kernel modules (usually device drivers) that may be required as part of your deployment. Finally, distribution vendors may create specific combinations of kernel versions, packages, and enhancements of their own. Later, in Chapters 5, 6, and 7, we will look at distributions, standards, and deployment processes to help you manage the details of this complexity.

Linux Kernel Development and Version Control

Linus Torvalds owns the registered trademark for Linux and, in a formal sense, he approves the release of new versions of the Linux kernel. As a practical matter, however, the center of the universe for Linux kernel development is the kernel.org community, which fosters an open and collaborative development process.

New kernel versions in development are issued an odd number for the sub-version number. Kernel versions 2.1.x, 2.3.x, and 2.5.x are all kernels that have been, or are, under development. You can think of these as unstable alpha and beta quality software with very frequent interim releases. Generally, no company would deploy a production system based on one of these development kernels. Kernel versions with even sub-numbers, such as 2.0.x, 2.2.x, and 2.4.x, are all released kernels considered ready for production. Figure 2–5 demonstrates this versioning system.

One of the key struggles to overcome when joining the world of Linux is the lack of a defined roadmap of the future, and the lack of committed release dates. In the traditional development world, roadmaps tend to define the functionality that will be included at specific points in the future. The fact that this map doesn't exist for Linux makes many managers uncomfortable.

After a kernel has been released and stabilized, Linus Torvalds will initiate a new development cycle (the next odd-numbered minor version will be announced). The kernel community will assemble to determine the list of features that will comprise the next release of the kernel. This

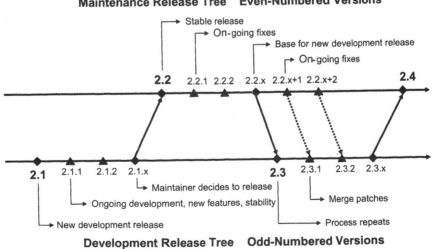

Figure 2–5 Linux kernel development lifecycle.

community of decision-makers is highly intelligent and very customer-focused. One of the greatest compliments a developer can receive is to have his or her software in production. This has the effect of driving high-quality contributions on the part of open source developers. The other phenomenon is to release when the community deems the system ready, not when some marketing department (or some "irrational" manager) says it is time to do so.

Oftentimes, companies release software due to perceived market and competitive pressures, as well as customer demand. This forces engineering departments to make unfavorable design and architectural trade-offs to meet top-down-imposed deadlines. The irony of this model is that, in many cases, the design and architectural tradeoffs end up adding development time and reducing the quality and functionality over the life of a system. Since the open source community is more motivated by delivering a quality system rather than by achieving an economic return, this negative cycle of development tends to be avoided. This does not imply that the community is oblivious to market needs and customer demands. Rather, it means that the design tradeoffs will tend to be more rational and with far fewer negative downstream effects. This software release cycle is a key reason that many open source projects are able to evolve at a far more rapid rate than their commercial counterparts and why they tend to be more stable.

The best way to influence the Linux feature set, accelerate the release of a new Linux kernel, or see a "roadmap" is very simple: get involved. The Linux development community operates under a code of respect and relationships. Get connected and participate in Linux development. This will be a win-win for you and the kernel community. Investing your resources in being an insider will give you an intimate understanding of how development is progressing and when releases are likely to happen. Your participation and influence will result in better planning on the part of your enterprise and a more leading-edge IT infrastructure. Even though Linux and other open source projects do not have a published roadmap, the very nature of open development gives you a very direct, inside view as to development progress. This view will very likely give you a better indication of the future than many published vendor roadmaps.

At some point, the kernel is pronounced as released to production and the next even-numbered minor version is assigned. Since development kernels are rarely tested in a production environment, it is not possible to work out all of the defects in the system. Although the community is well-recognized as one of the best at uncovering defects, in real life there is nothing better than a corporate production environment to completely shake out a system.

This shakeout process may uncover bugs that need to be fixed. Once Linus Torvalds releases a new even-numbered version of the Linux kernel, responsibility for its maintenance turns to Marcelo Tosatti (for many years, this role was the responsibility of Alan Cox). As companies deploy Linux and uncover defects, Marcelo approves the requisite changes to the kernel. Marcelo Tosatti and Linus Torvalds remain in constant contact. It is very important that Marcelo does not implement changes that would have negative long-term architectural impacts to the kernel. The bond of trust between Linus and Marcelo, and their willingness to accept suggestions from the Linux open source development community, is such that this condition is unlikely to occur.

As you encounter undesirable factors in your Linux deployment, the most productive way to work through them is with a strong bond to the community of kernel developers. It is typical for those who encounter defects in the kernel to not only report and document the problem, but to also submit a proposed fix (in the form of code changes) to Marcelo Tosatti. Of course, many companies will not have an IT staff with the size, experience, or knowledge required to be kernel experts. In these situations, companies will usually look to their Linux vendors for support. We will examine these support models in more detail in Chapter 8. The general end-user experience, however, is that problems are uncovered, diagnosed, and the resultant fixes published much faster than any commercial equivalent.

When a released kernel has stabilized to an acceptable degree, this stable kernel will be used as the foundation for the new development kernel and the cycle will repeat. When a production kernel and a development kernel are both in active development, Marcelo and Linus work together to ensure that synchronization is maintained.

Multi-Platform Support

One of the major strengths of Linux derives from the fact that it is already the most widely ported operating system.

Linus Torvalds originally developed the kernel as a project for school because he wanted a UNIX-like operating system for his new Intel 386-based PC. Portability was not a design objective. The kernel was tied very directly to the 386 microprocessor. But, as is often the case with open source projects, one can rarely predict how a project will evolve.

Many developers took on the task of porting the Linux kernel and adapting the structure to make Linux very portable.

Today, the Linux kernel development tree has both architecture-independent and architecture-dependent branches. The architecture-independent branches and code specific to the Intel x86 architecture are all maintained by Linus (components such as device drivers and file systems are maintained by others). The architecture-dependent branches for other microprocessors are maintained by separate groups of developers. When these developers encounter processor-specific issues, they are free to make the requisite changes to ensure proper functioning of the system. In some cases, changes are required to the architecture-independent components that also necessitate changes to the part under Linus' control. Maintainers of the kernel for alternate architectures work closely with Linus to plan these changes.

Mass-Market vs. Non-Mainstream Processors

Companies considering the deployment of Linux on non-mainstream microprocessors should consider additional factors in their decisions. Recall that one of the key benefits of Linux is that it applies commodity economics to the operating system. This joining of commodity microprocessors with Linux is what makes it such a viable and cost-attractive option for business.

Many consider one of the strengths of Linux to be its portability. This is true. There are cases when deploying Linux on proprietary or niche processors can be a viable and even desirable option; for example, when performance characteristics or specific feature sets are important. Linux on non-mainstream microprocessors is also a viable alternative when you need a migration path from your current installed base of proprietary processors toward an end goal of deploying only on mainstream processors. Some Linux distribution vendors are now making their Linux products available on non-mainstream processors, which may help this process. When evaluating alternative processors, consider the following:

- The core Linux development is currently done on the x86 architecture.
- Applications needed for your deployment may not be available, or will be delayed for a period of time from the base.
- ISVs may resist supporting their applications on anything but the mainstream. They may not have access to the resources needed to make their applications available or support them on alternative processor architectures.

- The open source development community will rarely have access to the resources needed to develop and test their specific components on all alternate architectures.
- Changes required in the architecture-dependent parts of the kernel may not make it upstream to their mainstream counterparts.
- Most device driver writers will be incapable of testing their devices on all alternative architectures.
- Trained Linux talent will rarely be familiar with Linux on alternative architectures.

While this is an important list to consider, you may still make the choice to deploy on non-mainstream processors. Today, in addition to the x86 (IA-32) processor architecture, the Linux kernel is available on these and other alternative architectures:

- AMD's Opteron
- HP's PA-RISC and Alpha
- IBM's PowerPC
- IBM's S/390
- Intel's Itanium Processor Family
- Motorola's 68K
- SUN's SPARC

In each case, the degree of support will vary. In most cases, however, full Linux distributions (discussed in Chapter 5) will be available. You can find more information on the support of Linux for a specific processor family in the reference section at the back of this book.

Linux on the Desktop

Deployment of Linux on the desktop is currently the source of much debate and controversy. By most market measures, Linux as an office productivity desktop has reached less than 2% (and by some measures less than 0.5%) penetration. The strongest proponents of Linux assert that it is only a matter of time before Linux begins to make significant inroads as a viable office desktop alternative. The main factors supporting this assertion are the popularity of Linux in many emerging countries throughout the world as well as the many government agencies also taking a serious look at Linux. Application availability, end-user friendliness, migration, and retraining costs make it difficult for most enterprises to consider deployments on their desktops. It is worth keeping close tabs on the market dynamics to see how these gaps are being addressed by the community and industry at large.

There are key market segments where Linux makes for a viable deployment alternative on the desktop today. The engineering desktop used by product development companies who traditionally used UNIX workstations continues to be a popular segment for Linux desktops. Markets dependent on high-end imaging applications, such as the entertainment industry and medical imaging markets, are also strong candidates for Linux deployments. Software developers are also attracted to the Linux desktop since they can develop for a familiar UNIX environment with their low-cost Linux PCs. Finally, transactional workstations used for specialized applications such as financial services also make for ideal Linux desktop solutions. All of these share a common heritage in UNIX workstations. Linux delivers a UNIX experience for the end-user with a cost profile similar to PC deployments.

The open source community has already delivered two primary desktop user interface alternatives: the GNOME desktop and the K Desktop Environment (or KDE). Think of these as the dashboard in your car. If you are familiar with UNIX desktops, GNOME and KDE are the equivalent of the Common Desktop Environment (CDE), delivered by the Open Group. Each desktop environment has its unique "look and feel," and sports a unique API. For CDE, the API was Motif; for GNOME it is GTK; and for KDE, it is Qt. The beauty of Linux is that, regardless of which desktop you choose, you can run applications based on any of these APIs. Your company can make the choice to standardize on one specific desktop environment or let the end-users choose and still be assured that applications will run.

There are also a number of office productivity suites available for the Linux desktop. The most popular are StarOffice, a proprietary solution offered by SUN and OpenOffice, an open source implementation of StarOffice maintained by SUN and a community of open source developers.

Vertical and Horizontal Scalability

The 2.4 kernel was a significant leap forward for multiprocessor (or "vertical") scalability. Depending on the application, Linux can now scale very well and industry and community groups continue to work on extending scalability. The Linux kernel is typically compiled to either be in a uniprocessor or multiprocessor configuration. A multiprocessor configuration is what enables vertical scalability. Prior to the 2.4 kernel being available, clustering (or "horizontal") scalability was the only way to achieve scalability. One of the most popular clustering technologies in development since 1994 is the Beowulf cluster (see the reference section at the end of this book for a link). Figure 2–6 depicts the difference between vertical and horizontal scalability:

Many applications based on traditional data processing now have a kernel and operating system that provide vertical scaling to address the vast majority of requirements. Those who require the massively parallel processing typically associated with high-performance computer clusters also have technology that has been evolving for more than eight years. Linus' school project has now reached, in a very short time, a level of usability and sophistication equal to that offered by commercial UNIX systems.

Embedded Linux

There are numerous companies specializing in delivering a Linux environment focused on embedded applications (vehicle controllers, TV set-top boxes, etc.). The ability to customize the Linux kernel makes it an ideal environment for embedded applications. It is possible to build a scaled down, limited functionality kernel that runs in one megabyte of random access memory (RAM).

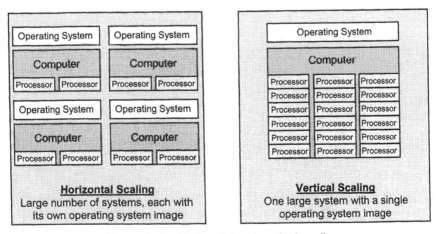

Figure 2–6 Horizontal and vertical scaling.

By license, Linux is freely copyable. Since many embedded applications involve the deployment of millions of units, eliminating the need for royalty fees based on volume makes Linux an attractive choice.

You can also build on and leverage the work of other companies specializing in embedded Linux kernels (Chapter 5 will outline some Linux distributions for embedded applications). If you have specialized or complex embedded requirements, you can build a custom embedded kernel or seek the services of companies specializing in the embedded market. Your choice will be dependent on your ability to support your own custom environment.

Summary

You can take off your propeller hat now, but you might want to keep it handy. This chapter is about as technical as it gets, but I will take the occasional detour through a few other difficult subjects. You have traversed through one of the most complex topics in computer science. Understanding what the Linux kernel is was one of the key foundations to understanding how a complete Linux system comes together and how you will deploy it in your organization. When we discuss Linux distributions in Chapter 5, you will understand how the kernel connects to the larger system.

In the next chapter, we will stretch your understanding of intellectual property law and examine a new paradigm in software development processes. Open source is what makes Linux and many other applications possible. Understanding how open source works and the legal foundation on which it is built is a prerequisite for deploying Linux.

Open Source— Navigating the Legal Path to Freedom

*L*inux's rapid rise has caused it to receive a great deal of industry and press hype. Linux is the single largest open source project, encompassing many hundreds of developers. It has demonstrated the true capabilities of open source. Therefore, as a technology leader for your company, you need to become an expert on open source. This new software development methodology and licensing model represents one of the newest opportunities and one of the greatest threats to your organization. It presents opportunity since it gives you new ways to lower costs and create competitive advantage. Open source also creates a threat by exposing your business to significant intellectual property risk. You need to care about open source because the odds are quite good that many developers in your organization are already using open source software. The odds are not as good that these same developers fully understand the risks to your company. Become the expert and take advantage of the opportunity while virtually eliminating the risks. The goals for this chapter are for you to understand:

- Freedom and open source
- The Open Source Definition
- Open source licenses, including the GPL
- Non-open source licenses often mistaken for open source
- Open source and U.S. cryptography export laws
- The open source development methodology

This chapter focuses on understanding open source and its legal dynamics. Part 3 of this book will include an in-depth discussion on the business processes associated with the use of open source software within your corporation, as well as a guide to help you decide when to implement the open source software that you have developed.

The Freedom to Be Open Source

Open source gets its roots from *free software*. When most people first hear the term "free software," they invariably jump to the conclusion that the software is without cost. This is not true. The word "free" when applied to software in this context is about freedom—meaning the freedom to copy, modify, and distribute the software. In principle, those freedoms require equal access to the source code. Richard Stallman is the author of the term "free software." He implemented important software for UNIX, licensed that software to the public under his GPL, and then created the Free Software Foundation (FSF) to promote this concept of freedom.

Following the model promoted by the FSF, when Linus Torvalds distributed Linux, he did so under the GPL free software license.

Other leaders of the free software movement, including Eric Raymond and Larry Augustin (among many others), were concerned about the confusion with the other meaning of the word "free" in the English language, "without cost." This confusion, they believed, was unnecessarily frightening larger software companies away from the development model underlying free software. Eric Raymond wrote his historic essay, "The Cathedral and the Bazaar" (later published as a collection of essays under that same title), to describe the creation of excellent software by communities of developers. To describe this software, he coined the term "open source" because it evoked no economic model, yet it recognized that open access to the source code was essential to this development process.

These leaders also recognized that the success of open source depended on a clear description of what was allowable in an open source license. The Debian community's project leader at the time, Bruce Perens, had already worked to define a social contract with the free software community (I discuss Debian in more detail in Chapter 5, but for now, suffice it to say that Debian is a community–developed, open source Linux distribution). Bruce and other leaders of the open source movement agreed to adopt this social contract as the official Open Source Definition (OSD). Bruce is therefore credited as the primary author of the OSD.

It should be noted that those who subscribe to the pure notion of free software, including Richard Stallman, do not agree with the change of name to "open source." The reason for this will become clear later in this chapter when I discuss the GPL and other "copyleft" licenses.

The Open Source Definition

In general terms, an open source license protects the rights of anyone, anywhere, for any purpose whatsoever to use, copy, modify, and distribute (sell *or* give away) software. In practice, this requires open access to the source code.

These essential rights are codified more formally in an official OSD, published by the Open Source Initiative (OSI), a non-profit corporation. The open source community recognizes the OSD as the guide to what is truly an open source license. Licenses that comply with the provisions of the OSD necessarily provide the essential rights listed above.

It is very important to understand that the OSD is *not* itself a license. Bruce Perens, the author of the initial version of the OSD, refers to it as a specification that actual licenses must comply with so that software distributed under the licenses can be legitimately "open source." For the complete, detailed text of the OSD, check the reference section at the end of this book for the link.

The OSI created a certification mark to serve as an indicator of a legitimate open source license; when you see "OSI Certified" on a software package, you can be assured that the license under which that software is distributed complies with the OSD.

There is no corresponding standard definition (or rule set) for proprietary licenses. Every company develops its own. Attorneys must review the terms of each such proprietary license to ensure that the rights and obligations it contains are acceptable.

In the past few years, many people have asked me what "open source" really means. What I have found helpful is to summarize the specific provisions of the published OSD. Below is such a summary. If you want a more comprehensive definition of each provision, visit the OSI Web site (*www.opensource.org*). All of these provisions must apply for the license to be open source and for software distributed under that license to be OSI Certified. The OSD provisions are:

1. **Free redistribution**—An open source license cannot prevent a licensee from redistributing the software for free. It must be entirely up to each licensee to determine whether or what to charge for copies. It is common for providers of open source software to charge a fee for the media, the manuals, and support offerings of an open source software product. As a practical matter, this provision usually results in free or low-cost software.

2. **Source code**—The source code to the program must be made available. In most cases, the source code will be included with the binary (the executable program), but it is not a requirement. However, if the source is not provided with the binary, it must be available for download (or on other media) without charge. As a practical matter, because the source code is available, anyone (or rather, anyone with the requisite skills) can fix bugs or enhance the software.

3. **Derived works**—The license must allow the software to be modified and for that modified software to be redistributed. If you acquire open source software, you are free to change it, and you are free to redistribute your changed version.

4. **Integrity of the author's source code**—In the normal course of development within the open source community, the master source tree is usually controlled by a "maintainer." There may be cases where the maintainer will reject changes to the official source tree, but a programmer will still want to distribute changes. From a licensing and recognition standpoint, there needs to be a clear way to separate the official source from any modifications. The "integrity" provision of the OSD ensures that you know who is responsible for the source code you are using. Thus, the author gets clear credit (or blame) for his or her work and doesn't get credit/blame for someone else's modifications. Some open source licenses require modifications to be made through patches, so that the original source is distributed unmodified, and then the modifications are provided in a separate patch file. The two are combined at build time to provide new, working software.

5. **No discrimination against person or groups**—An open source license cannot prevent the use or redistribution of the software (and its source) to anyone or any group. No matter how much we may despise certain users of software, this clause prevents any

restrictions. (For example, you cannot prevent terrorists from using your software.) In business terms, this also means that you cannot prevent a competitor from using or redistributing your software or its source code.

6. **No discrimination against fields of endeavor**—This provision prevents an open source licensor from controlling or limiting the way the software is used. A licensor cannot impose his or her political, social, and cultural values on the licensees of the software. An open source license cannot prevent commercialization of the software.

7. **Distribution of license**—In the open source model, the open source license is the only license that the licensor can impose. There can be no requirement to sign a non-disclosure agreement or execute a second license (such as a patent license) to obtain the software.

8. **License must not be specific to a product**—Open source software cannot be restricted to use with specific other products. For example, open source software cannot be limited to use with Linux.

9. **License must not contaminate other software**—For the license to comply with the OSD, it cannot force its license terms on other software distributed with it. This encourages companies to distribute both open source and proprietary software on the same CD or other medium.

These nine rules guide all open source licenses. As you can see, the focus is on freedom and ensuring that any license that considers itself to be open source adheres to the spirit of freedom.

Intellectual Property and Reciprocity

Some open source licenses impose a burden of reciprocity upon the licensee. It is essential for you to understand the implications of these reciprocity provisions on your own intellectual property.

But first, what is reciprocity and why do so many members of the free software and open source community insist upon it in their licenses? Reciprocity provisions generally require you to license back under an equivalent open source license—to the licensor and everyone else—all derivative works you create from the original software. The license under which Linux is made available to you, the GPL, contains such a reciprocity provision.

The FSF created a special word to describe reciprocity in their GPL. They call it "copyleft" to indicate the relationship of that term to the law of "copyright." Copyleft is a general method for making a program free software and requiring all modified and extended versions of the program to be free software as well. To copyleft a program, the software is first copyrighted, and then the software is distributed under a license, a legal instrument that gives everyone the rights to use, modify, and redistribute the program's code or any program derived from it but only if the distribution terms are unchanged. Thus, the code and freedoms become legally inseparable. (Remember, the word "free" doesn't mean "at no cost"; this concept of freedom relates to the rights guaranteed by the OSD discussed earlier.)

Reciprocity (or copyleft) allows the creator of an original piece of software to benefit from your improvements just as you benefited from his or her providing you the source code that made those improvements possible. Contributors of open source software are encouraged to give their software away for free because they get better free software in return.

Reciprocity obligations don't arise by the *use* of software; they only arise when the modified (and/or improved) software is distributed. So if you are using Linux as an operating system on your computers, but are not distributing Linux outside of your company, reciprocity obligations from the Linux license don't apply to you. Reciprocity obligations, furthermore, only apply when you modify the original program—in copyright law terms, when you create a derivative work. So if you merely distribute Linux to your customers just as you received it, reciprocity obligations from the Linux license don't apply to you.

If you modify Linux and distribute your modified version to others, you must license those modifications—including the source code—to everyone under the terms of the GPL. This is the only situation in which the reciprocity obligations of the Linux license apply to you. But it may be an important situation to you. When you modify software (including Linux) that you receive from others, you should consult an intellectual property attorney to determine whether you are creating a derivative work. Under a reciprocal open source license, you must give your derivative works to everyone under the same (or an equivalent) open source license.

Dual-Licensing and Copyright Ownership

Any copyright owner can license his or her copyrighted software under more than one license. Each licensee, then, can choose whether to accept the software under the terms of one or the other license.

For some open source software, the licensor allows you to elect to license the software under either a reciprocal open source license (like the GPL) or under a commercial license for which royalties must be paid. Such dual-licensing marketing strategies were developed in response to those customers who were unwilling to accept reciprocity requirements and were willing to pay to avoid them.

Linux is not available under a dual-license, but other important open source software that runs under Linux is. For example, Hans Reiser makes his file system, ReiserFS, available under more than one license. This allows ReiserFS to be used by the Linux operating system under the provisions of the GPL. However, Hans also has the ability to license his file system under a proprietary license. Developers of other operating systems work with Hans to make his file system available. The difference is that Hans can charge a fee for his work and the developer(s) can create an effective support structure for the file system. This is one example of many. Figure 3–1 demonstrates the flow of implementing a dual-license model.

To control licensing alternatives, open source developers often request that contributors assign them their copyrights in the enhanced software. That way, the original developer has the right to decide on the licensing strategy for the enhanced version. Linus Torvalds doesn't require the assignment of copyright when enhancements are made to Linux, but the FSF will accept copyright assignments so that it has a large body of open source work it can defend.

Some contributors refuse to assign their copyrights to anyone else. The management and accounting of copyright ownership is one of the major headaches for an open source project.

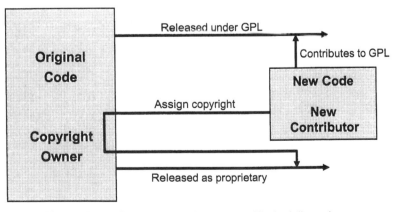

Figure 3–1   Copyright assignments with dual–licensing.

Licenses—Open Source and Non-Open Source

With an understanding of the OSD, reciprocity, and some of the dual-license issues associated with software, we can now look at some actual licenses. This section begins with a list of open source licenses. This section will also explain in detail the two most significant copyleft licenses, the GPL and LGPL.

Open Source Licenses

Table 3–1 outlines some of the most popular or significant open source licenses that have been approved by the OSI. You and your personnel can subscribe to an announcement list to keep track of new licenses approved by the OSI. It is interesting to note that the texts of the licenses are *not* governed by an open source license. If the text of a license can be modified, then there would not be a real requirement to comply with the license.

Table 3–1   Popular Open Source Licenses

License	Copyleft?	Comments
Apache Software License	No	This license is used by the Apache Web Server. It is a license similar to MIT and BSD. The major addition to this license was its express notice that the Apache trademark was not licensed along with the software. Thus, if you modify and distribute changed versions of the Apache code, you cannot call your changed program "Apache."
Artistic License	No	This license was developed for the Perl language. It is generally considered to be a confusing license with many loopholes that seem to contradict each other in their intent. These contradictions cause most to avoid using this license and use the GPL or the MIT license instead.

(continued)

License	Copyleft?	Comments
BSD License	No	The BSD license is very popular due to the fact that you can take BSD code, modify and distribute your changes, and you don't have to publish the source code of your modifications. The BSD license allows you to make the code private and then distribute it under a proprietary license. Although this license appears attractive, some of the core attributes of the GPL that cause a communal development process are lost. An early version of the BSD license required you to give credit to the University of California every time you used code under its license. This "advertising clause" made it incompatible with the GPL. The current version of the BSD license has dropped this clause.
GNU General Public License (GPL)	Yes	See the later discussion on the GPL. This is the license used for the Linux kernel. Most, but not all, open source software projects use this license.
GNU Lesser General Public License (LGPL)	Yes	See the later discussion on the LGPL. Similar to the GPL, but allows you to link non-free (as in freedom) software to LGPL code. However, modifications to the LGPL code itself must be returned if the modified version is distributed.
IBM Public License	Yes	A commercial "copyleft" license similar to the Mozilla Public License (see below) that includes extra indemnification provisions

(continued)

Table 3.1   *(continued)*

License	Copyleft?	Comments
IBM Public License *(continued)*		such that if someone makes claims about the capabilities of the original work, or any derived work, those claims are the sole responsibility of the one making the claims. Any contributor in the chain of original and derived works cannot be held responsible for any of the claims.
Mozilla Public License (MPL)	Yes	Mozilla is the open source version of the Netscape Navigator Web browser released by Netscape (now part of AOL). The MPL is an off-shoot of the Netscape Public License (NPL). See Table 3–2 for a description of the NPL. The MPL was created by Netscape to overcome some of the restrictions of the NPL. The MPL was the first major commercial open source license, and many other licenses, including the IBM Public License and others from commercial software companies, are derived from it.
MIT License	No	A very simple license that has virtually no restrictions on how the source is used. The only requirement is that the text of the license must be included in all copies, or substantial portions, of the software. If you simply want to apply ownership to your code, but let it be used without any conditions, this is a good license.
Python License	No	Python is an interpreted, object-oriented programming language very popular within the Linux and

(continued)

License	Copyleft?	Comments
Python License *(continued)*	No	UNIX communities. The Python license is specific to Python, but is very liberal. You simply need to quote the Python license in any derivative works.
Qt Public License (QPL)	Yes	Qt is a development library at the core of the KDE desktop environment. Qt is similar to Motif in functionality. The Qt license requires any software program that links to the library to make source code available. Qt is similar to the LGPL with one major difference: the LGPL allows commercial, private code to use the linked LGPL library whereas the Qt license does not. Qt is also a good example of an open source license that requires modifications be distributed through patches.
SUN Industry Standards Source License (SISSL)	No	SISSL has been applied by SUN to the Open Office project for those areas that apply to the XML file format specification and the Open Office API specification. This license was created to ensure that the standards applied to the Open Office file format and API remain open and royalty-free. It also ensures that any extensions or enhancements to the standard are made public through the publication of the source code of a reference implementation. Licenses like SISSL are used when it is important to provide the freedom of open source development along with some control over the standards that the open source code implements.

Although this table lists the most popular open source licenses, we need to take a more detailed look at primary copyleft licenses such as the GPL and LGPL.

The GPL and LGPL

The most talked about open source license is the GPL, or the *GNU general public license*. The GPL was authored by Richard Stallman as a way to ensure that the freedom of source code he was creating did not get abused by others (see Appendix C for the full text of the GPL). By simply making software open and public, Richard understood there was a real danger that others could take that software and reuse it in restrictive and proprietary ways. Richard wanted to ensure a *quid-pro-quo*. If you benefit from open software, then any changes or contributions you make should benefit others as well. The GPL ensures that this chain of freedom is never broken. The license requires that any modifications you make to GPL code and that you distribute ***must*** be made available to the community. The GPL was the first "copyleft" license. Figure 3–2 outlines two source trees, one GPL and one proprietary, and how the flow of the source needs to be considered.

Unfortunately, some have incorrectly interpreted the GPL to mean that anything that touches running GPL code must also be GPL. This is completely false. The best example of this is the Linux operating system. The Linux kernel is licensed under the GPL. Today, there are many commercial applications (e.g., Oracle) that are available on Linux that are not GPL. Part 3 will go into the details of writing software that is closely connected to the GPL without forcing the GPL on the source base.

The other close cousin to the GPL is the LGPL, or *lesser GNU general public license*. The LGPL was created to solve the problem of using libraries licensed under the GPL. The GPL forces any commercial application that uses shared libraries licensed under the GPL and that is distributed

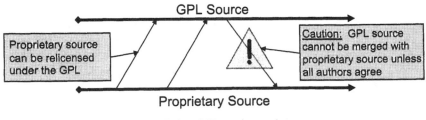

Figure 3–2   Mixing GPL and proprietary source.

to also be GPL, but this doesn't apply to the LGPL. For example, in the Linux environment, many applications are dependent on the core system runtime library, *glibc*. By licensing *glibc* under the LGPL, commercial applications can link to it without concern about an application being required to be licensed under the GPL. The LGPL can be a good solution when you want to create open source software, but still allow commercially licensed software to use your technology. But be careful. When changing the code within LGPL source, the normal GPL rules apply. Enhancements and changes to the library itself, when distributed, must be licensed under the LGPL. Since the LGPL is most often applied to libraries, the LGPL is often referred to the *library GNU general public license*. Figure 3–3 shows the connection of proprietary software to LGPL software and how both combined deliver a complete application.

The LGPL is still widely used, but has created much confusion. As a result, Richard Stallman now advises against using it and to use a special extension clause to the GPL:

> *"As a special exception, if you link this library with other files to produce an executable, this library does not by itself cause the resulting executable to be covered by the GNU General Public License. This exception does not however invalidate any other reasons why the executable file might be covered by the GNU General Public License."*

While the GPL and LGPL are probably the most known and likely the most used open source licenses, there are many others. Some of these

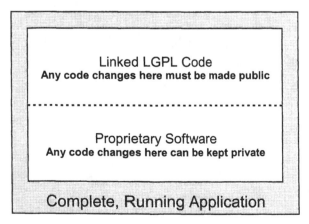

Figure 3–3   Linking proprietary software with LGPL code.

licenses existed before the OSD was publicized; some were created to be less restrictive than the GPL. Since there are already more than 30 approved licenses and creating new ones will generally only serve to confuse, you should avoid creating a new one if at all possible.

The GPL and Linux Kernel Modules

As described in Chapter 2, one of the most significant enhancements to version 2.0 of the Linux kernel was support for kernel modules. Kernel modules provide a way for the kernel to be separated into functional components. Rather than compiling device drivers or extended functionality directly into the kernel, modules can be "bolted" on to the kernel at runtime, as needed. When a kernel module is loaded, it becomes part of the kernel. Figure 3–4 is the same picture from Chapter 2, but includes a reference to the open source nature of kernel modules as it relates to the Linux kernel itself.

From a GPL license perspective, this creates a special problem. Is a module bound by the terms of the GPL? In one sense, it is part of the kernel and should be bound by the terms of the GPL. In another sense, it is distinct code and should be exempt from the terms of the GPL. This gray

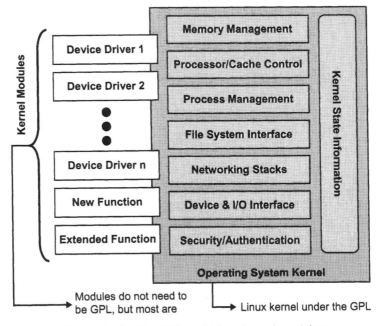

Figure 3–4   The GPL and Linux kernel modules.

area created a hot debate within the community. Linus Torvalds provided the needed clarity by declaring that kernel modules would not be bound by the GPL terms of the Linux kernel if they restricted themselves to standard interfaces. Binary only modules cannot implement new system calls (system calls are APIs that developers use to interact with the kernel) or rewrite existing portions of the kernel. Although this appears to create a loophole in the GPL as it relates to the Linux kernel, exploiting it is ill-advised since Linus is not the sole copyright owner of the kernel. It is widely accepted that if kernel developers begin extending the functionality of the kernel by exploiting this "kernel module loophole," the loophole will be closed, perhaps through a revision of the GPL. Therefore, don't exploit this loophole to modify the Linux kernel.

The LGPL and Class Inheritance

The LGPL is a license mostly used for libraries. It allows proprietary code to use the functionality of libraries without being forced into GPL rules. There is another special case associated with the extension of class libraries. As shown in Figure 3–5, object-oriented languages such as C++ are built on hierarchies of classes.

Each extension of the hierarchy provides new functionality built on the original base class. Whereas the LGPL rules are clear when it comes to using the functionality of a library, the rules are not as clear when it comes to extending the functionality of a class library.

As of this writing, the debate on this topic is ongoing. Since there is currently no clear answer, the LGPL should be avoided (or used with caution) when extending the functionality of an existing class library if you need to maintain proprietary code.

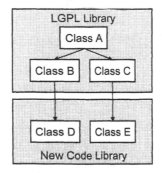

Does this new code library need to be LGPL?

Figure 3–5   Class inheritance and the LGPL.

Non-Open Source Licenses

There are a few "non-open source licenses," or licenses that do not comply with the OSD but that satisfy many of its requirements. Remember that just because source code has been made available to you, the license may not comply with the OSD. These non-open source licenses are usually created to solve very specific business issues. In some cases, a company may not have the rights to license the code, but wants to benefit from communal development. In other cases, it may be appropriate to make source available to help other developers debug an application. It is not possible to present an exhaustive list of non-open source licenses. Most of the licenses that provide access to source code but don't fit the OSD fall into one of the following situations:

1. The owner wanted to give the ability to debug an application dependent on a development library. For example, Microsoft distributes source code to most of its foundation classes (MFC). This allows a developer to trace his or her application through Microsoft source. Microsoft does not currently have a true open source license, however.
2. The individual or company does not own complete rights. In many cases, someone would like to apply an open source license but is restricted from doing so because of contracts with other third parties. In most of these cases, a new license is created that is specific to the company and/or product.
3. The individual or company wants feedback from a development community without giving up intellectual property (IP) rights. There are cases where a company might want to provide access to source code to get the benefit of feedback and peer review from a development community. Any changes and rights must be returned to the company. Microsoft's shared source license fits into this category. This type of license has generated significant ill will within the open source development community. However, it may be appropriate if your business model is completely dependent on software license revenue and an alternate business model is not possible.

Table 3–2 lists some significant non-open source licenses you should be aware of. These licenses do not meet the requirements of the OSD.

Table 3–2 Significant Non-Open Source Licenses

License	Comments
Microsoft Shared Source	Microsoft's shared source license provides access to source, but requires you to return changes you make back to Microsoft. Microsoft gains all the rights for the changes and/or enhancements that you make. Check the reference section at the back of this book for a link to Microsoft's shared source licensing page. The shared source license provides no redistribution rights.
Netscape Public License (NPL)	The NPL is specific to Netscape. Netscape created the NPL due to encumberments they had with third parties. Until Mozilla provided a true open source code base for the browser, NPL gave Netscape a way to release the code and gain community support, while still meeting its contractual requirements with third parties.
SUN Community Source License	The SUN Community Source License is also a form of a shared source license. Code can be contributed to enhance a product or technology, but any work done must comply with SUN's definition of a particular standard. Redistribution also requires royalty payments back to SUN Microsystems. As noted in the previous table, SUN also has a different licensing model (SISSL) that fits with the OSD. Make sure you know which of SUN's licenses you are bound to.

These are important licenses to consider. Keep in mind that new licenses are created on a regular basis and make sure you have a clear understanding that a license must meet all the rules of the OSD or it is not an open source-approved license.

Export and Cryptography

Software that is open source must still comply with the laws regarding export control. This is particularly important for software that includes cryptographic capabilities, because the U.S. and some other countries impose restrictions on the export of such software.

Because open source software is so readily copied and distributed worldwide, no open source license can explicitly require compliance with U.S. law. Such a license would conflict with Clause 5 of the OSD ("No discrimination against persons or groups). An open source license cannot excuse compliance with the law. Anyone who writes software and distributes it is responsible for reviewing the export control laws of his or her country and following those laws.

For open source Linux distributions, this presented a special problem. Originally, the only way to deliver full cryptographic capabilities in Linux was to do it outside the U.S. For some time, certain "crypto" software, for example Secure Sockets Layer- (SSL-) enhanced Web servers, needed to be developed and downloaded from sources outside the U.S.

Recent changes in U.S. export law allow open source software containing cryptographic code to be exported. A simple notification to the relevant government agencies is all that is required. This provides an incentive for all cryptographic software to be open sourced as a way to circumvent current restrictions. Details are available at the Bureau of Industry and Security (*www.bis.doc.gov*). Search for the current Export License Exception Chart and look for license exception TSU—§740.13.

Since it is always possible for rules and restrictions to change, much of the cryptographic software within the open source community is developed and maintained outside the U.S. Therefore, any changes in U.S. export law should have little impact on Linux and any other open source applications.

Open Source Development Methodology

While the licensing models usually get all the attention when it comes to open source, what is really interesting is the development methodology associated with it. The real beauty of open source is not the license; it is the process.

This description of the open source development methodology applies to many projects. The specifics will change depending on the size and use of the project. Eric Raymond's essay (and book), *The Cathedral and the Bazaar*, details Eric's discovery and test of the process. Eric was astonished that the process seemed to violate every known rule of traditional software development (the cathedral model), yet worked. Eric's paper (very well worth the read) outlines Eric's discovery (the bazaar model) while creating and running an open source project. Here are the key elements of the methodology without running a project through it. The point is for you to understand the terms, the tools, the players, and the process.

License

While the development process is not about the license, it is the license that provides the boundary conditions that make the process work. These conditions establish a foundation that ensures communal and collaborative development. Since the GPL, LGPL, and other licenses that contain a reciprocity requirement provide that changes and modifications be returned to the community, this is the foundation that ensures collaborative development.

Styles

The open source development methodology can also be referred to as the Linux development method. Linus Torvalds deserves the credit for demonstrating that this bazaar style of development has worked, and worked well. The method has been adapted to a number of styles:

1. **Company**—In this style, a corporation takes the lead for a development project. This usually means assigning paid developers to the project, funding the infrastructure to host the development, and being the overall maintainer of the project. Even with this style, the company will often assign one developer as the overall maintainer. HP, IBM, SUN, and many other large corporations all lead open source projects.
2. **Foundation**—A foundation is often created as a means to fund a large project. Companies and individuals interested in making sure a project is successful can donate funds to this non-profit organization. There are cases where a company has taken the lead for a project, but a foundation has also been established. This is usually because the company that has taken the lead does

not have the financial resources to fund the project on its own. The GNOME Foundation is a good example of this development style. Many companies fund the GNOME Foundation; however, Ximian is the corporation that has taken the lead to "productize" the GNOME desktop.

3. **Committee**—The committee style is also used for large projects. Committees are usually set up to provide a forum for decision-making. This usually means a more consensus-driven decision-making approach rather than the more common approach of one single maintainer making decisions. The GCC (GNU C/C++ Compiler) compilers most often used on Linux are managed this way.

4. **Individual**—Small projects are typically run by individuals. There are literally thousands of these projects. Many are hosted on a site called SourceForge, although lately, more and more projects are moving to Savannah which is a free software repository hosted by the GNU project. These projects will often involve fewer than five developers. Many of these projects also evolve simply because a hacker needed a solution to a specific problem and could not find one.

5. **Linux kernel**—This special style is the one used by Linus Torvalds for the largest open source development project. Linus has evolved this model over the years and it is based on a hierarchy of trust within the kernel development community. In Part 3, I will outline a theoretical model of how the Linux kernel development process could be applied within your corporation.

6. **GNU**—This style of development is not well-known, and most prefer to use the styles listed previously. The GNU style uses conventional development methodologies (which you will learn as "cathedral" development later) to produce free software.

Attributes

Attributes are a set of characteristics that most open source projects have. This set of characteristics is the foundation of an important culture that drives community behavior. Most open source projects share the following set of attributes:

1. **Maintainer**—Most projects are run by a maintainer. The maintainer is the individual who initiated the project, or who was assigned by a previous maintainer. The maintainer accepts/rejects submissions, applies patches, monitors defects, and interacts with other projects where needed. Open source projects typically have an orderly handoff from one maintainer to another. When a developer loses interest in a project (or no longer has the time to devote to it), he or she will pass the torch along to a new maintainer. The new maintainer is typically selected from a list of individuals who have made significant contributions to the project. Maintainers are always volunteers. There are cases where the maintainer is a committee established for the project. Also, when a project is driven by a company, the maintainer may be a group of individuals within that company.

2. **Respect**—Built over time, and by ongoing contributions, respect for the individual is paramount in the open source development community. If a developer attempts to contribute poor code, he or she will be quickly notified by members of the community—the community tends to be equally vocal with praise and criticism. Continuous, high-quality contributions will build respect over time. A maintainer (such as Linus Torvalds) will more readily accept contributions from someone he or she knows well and has a history of good, solid code. Contributions from an unknown will be carefully examined and critiqued before being accepted. Poor contributions will cause a developer to get shunned by the community.

3. **Individuals as maintainers**—Even though companies will often fund and promote open source projects, the maintainer is often an individual. Even if the maintainer changes companies, he or she may continue as the official maintainer of the code. In some cases, a change of companies means a change of priorities and the maintainer will pass the torch. People always think of Linus as the maintainer of the Linux kernel, not Transmeta, Linus' current employer, nor any future employer he may have.

4. **Tools**—All developers within a community are used to working with a well-established infrastructure with common development tools. For example, CVS is a well-accepted source management tool and Bugzilla is most often used for defect tracking.

It should be noted that while CVS is a widely accepted source management tool, it is not used for the Linux kernel. The Linux kernel relies on "patch." SourceForge, and now Savannah, provide a development infrastructure and repositories for open source and free software.

5. **Release early and often**—One of the fundamental differences between what Eric calls the cathedral development style and the open source bazaar development style is the notion of frequent development releases available for peer review, which exists in the bazaar style. This rapid and ongoing release cycle allows a team of developers to quickly recognize defects and address them early in the development process. Developers frequently use the early development release versions in their daily work, giving them thorough use testing. This attribute is often noted as the reason why open source products are developed more quickly than traditional products, and with much higher quality.

6. **Release for production when ready**—As described in Chapter 2, most companies release software (either for internal use or for sale) based on a timeline driven by external factors such as market and business pressures that have little to do with how ready the project is for release. In the open source development process, the community generally releases to production when the maintainer thinks the product is ready. Many businesses are uncomfortable with the lack of solid roadmap when dealing with open source projects. However, those who accept this immediately begin to benefit from higher quality software, fewer patches, and a better system architecture.

The combinations of these open source attributes with the various development styles represent an impressive communal development process. It takes time and courage to adapt a company's culture to this development style, but the benefits have been proven—just look at Linux and the Apache Web Server, two large open source projects that run a vast portion of the Internet!

Summary

You have now been versed in the details of open source and how it relates to free software. We examined the OSD in detail, looked at a number of licenses that comply with the OSD as well as some that do not, and finally, we looked at how the community runs a bazaar-style development process and some of the key attributes of projects within the community. In Part 3, we will extend our discussion of open source to the connections within a corporation and answer the following questions:

1. What are the business risks associated with the GPL and LGPL and how should they be managed?
2. How does open source affect established business models?
3. How can companies benefit from the bazaar development style?
4. How can companies work on open source projects?
5. What are the key business processes affected by open source development?

In the next chapter, we will look at some of the key communities and organizations within the open source community and the roles they play.

Communities
and Organizations

*O*pen source represents a collection of communities. Chapter 3 described some of the various ways in which projects can be run, from company-run projects to foundations. There are also a number of other organizations that exist in support of Linux and the open source movement. Having a deeper understanding of all the communities out there will give you a sense of how large the movement truly is. There are also complex interactions between many communities that you can only begin to understand if you have visibility to the larger whole.

This chapter outlines some of the most significant communities. I will start with the Linux kernel community, look at some of the major open source foundations, and finally, describe some industry organizations. A link is included to all of the organizations both here and in the reference section at the end of the book. It is not possible for this chapter to present a list of all possible groups, communities, foundations, and organizations. However, it is more than enough to get you started. In many cases, I could write a complete chapter, or even a book, for some of these communities. The intent here is to give you a view of what is out there, not to give you a comprehensive view of each and every project. This will also give you an inside look at some key open source projects that are giving their commercial counterparts a run for their money. If you are developing commercial applications, take note: You might be the one facing market erosion next.

Reading this chapter in detail is not required. At a minimum, you should scan this chapter and read the detail of the communities that you think are relevant to your business. Also, take some time to look through some of the communities that you might not be familiar with. Then, refer back to this chapter on occasion when you are looking for a connection point to a specific community.

Linux

As you learned in Chapters 1 and 2, Linux is a kernel. The kernel community comprises a number of groups focused on the core of the kernel proper, processor-specific work, and finally those that work on extensions to the kernel such as file systems and other device drivers.

Kernel

http://www.kernel.org/

The center of the kernel universe starts at *kernel.org*. This group of engineers focuses on the deepest and most complex aspects of software development. Playing here is not for the faint of heart. You will find a very sparse Web site focused on the developer. This community, like many others, operates on the basis of email conversations through reflectors (email sent to one address is automatically forwarded to all subscribers). The email traffic is very high, and only those who are dedicated to kernel development should connect to this community.

Processors

x86 (IA-32)
The IA-32 processor family does not have a different community since it is at the core of all kernel development. Simply follow the link for primary kernel development.

Itanium Processor Family (IPF, also known as IA-64)
http://www.linuxia64.org/

IPF is widely believed to be the successor to the IA-32 family of processors. This will not happen overnight. For the immediate future, IA-32 will continue to provide price/performance leadership for low-end systems. Look to IPF to take an early lead in higher end computing, and to gradually take over as the dominant processor as applications begin to demand 64-bit computing and a commodity-driven ecosystem evolves around the architecture.

Linux for IPF began as a project primarily driven by David Mosberger and Stephane Eranian at HP Labs. Intel and other companies who were under confidential disclosure requirements from Intel were also doing work in this space. Shortly after the project began, this group of companies, which included HP, Intel, SGI, IBM, and others, formed a consortium known as the Trillian group. Trillian allowed companies to work on Linux support for Itanium without disclosing the specifics of Itanium to the general public. When Intel finally released Itanium to the industry at large, the Trillian group was disbanded and the code for Linux on IPF was available as open source.

An IPF simulator is available for the IA-32 processor family. The wonderful thing about this is that it allows developers to use their low-cost laptops and desktops for all their development for Linux on IPF. There are a number of other tools available at the official Linux IPF Web site.

David continues his role today as the maintainer of the Linux/IPF kernel and is one of a few individuals on the short list to succeed Linus. David also represents a good example of where the maintainer of the project is an individual, not the company.

Alpha

http://www.linuxalpha.org/

The Alpha processor is well-liked within Linux circles. In fact, for a long time, Alpha was the preferred processor for Linux in high-performance computing applications.

The Alpha Linux Organization hosts this community. Some distribution providers have been providing support for the Alpha implementation. However, prior to its acquisition by HP, Compaq had announced an impending end of life for Alpha and has committed to the IPF for its future. Much of the Alpha IP is now owned by Intel.

PowerPC

http://www.linuxppc.org/
http://www.linuxppc.com/

IBM and Motorola have both produced PowerPC. The PowerPC community is largely focused on providing Linux support for Mac computers running the PowerPC microprocessor. There are also a number of IBM systems supported. Some distributions also create versions for this architecture.

PA-RISC

http://www.parisc-linux.org/

PA-RISC is the processor family developed by HP. HP has also made significant investments in the IPF and is the co-inventor along with Intel. HP is evolving PA-RISC to IPF as its strategic microprocessor for the future. The Puffin Group, a small startup company, initiated the Linux kernel port to the PA-RISC processor. HP provided assistance in the form of development support and documentation. The Puffin Group was acquired by LinuxCare and they now host most of the development activities with Linux on PA-RISC.

File Systems

Linux supports a wide variety of file systems. Generically, file systems define how data is stored, indexed, and retrieved from disk. The most common file system available for Linux is the ext2 file system. If you acquire one of the standard Linux distributions, this is likely what will be there. However, there are a number of reasons why you might choose an alternate. In some cases you might want to share disks between different systems, and therefore, they need to share a common structure. In other cases, you might have specific performance or reliability requirements that will dictate a specific file system. You should also perform a number of tests using your specific application workloads to decide which file system is best for you. Here are some of the other major file systems to look for:

EXT

http://e2fsprogs.sourceforge.net/ext2.html

As I mentioned, the ext2 file system is the one most often shipped with Linux distributions. Ext3 represents journaling extensions to the ext2 file system. Ext3 is not a file system, but rather provides journaling capabilities to ext2 while maintaining backward compatibility. See the next section for a discussion of journaling.

IBM JFS

http://oss.software.ibm.com/developer/opensource/jfs/

Journaling file systems add a significant amount of resiliency and reliability to operating systems. During the normal operation of a system, there is a significant amount of disk storage and retrieval taking place.

Since disk storage is relatively slow, all systems use a number of techniques to accelerate the availability and storage of information. This acceleration usually takes the form of temporary storage of disk information in the main system memory. However, if there is a disk failure in the middle of all this activity, then the integrity of the information on the disk can be compromised. Journaling file systems such as JFS, ReiserFS, ext3, and others use a number of sophisticated techniques to ensure that data storage is not compromised during failures. The other aspect of these file systems is that they allow for the very rapid recovery of systems in the event of failures.

With the availability of a number of journaling systems, Linux has overcome what many considered to be a very significant limitation of the operating system.

XFS

http://oss.sgi.com/projects/xfs/

XFS is a journaling file system released under the GPL by SGI. All file systems will perform with different characteristics depending on the application. The XFS file system is generally a good choice when large files are used, and when your need is to keep the number of accesses to disk to a minimum to read these large files. Visit the XFS home page for details on the features of XFS.

ReiserFS

http://www.namesys.com/

Hans Reiser is the creator of the ReiserFS file system, a high-performance journaling file system available under the GPL. If you recall our discussion on dual-licensing, Hans also licenses his file system to commercial operating system vendors. This feature may allow you to use the same file system technology and share storage between Linux and many other UNIX deployments you might have.

Device Support

It is not possible to list the communities for each and every device out there. The best way to find support for your specific device is to check the supported device list for your distribution. When we discuss Linux distributions in detail in Chapter 5, I will talk more about how distributions provide device support.

Web Services and Application Servers

I have already discussed the role of the Apache Web Server in the explosive growth of Linux. But Apache is not alone, and the work of Apache is no longer confined to the simple Web server. The Web has also evolved from providing static content such as publications to more dynamic content, which is usually associated with database interactions. Additionally, we have seen the evolution into e-commerce, business logic, and most recently, full-blown Web services. There are a number of open source communities dedicated to providing offerings in this ever-evolving space. Keep in mind that many of these are not dedicated to Linux; many of these open source capabilities are available for operating systems other than Linux. Here are a few to keep a close eye on:

Apache

http://www.apache.org/

The Apache Foundation was formed as a non-profit corporation to further the development of not only the core Web server, but all of the dynamic services evolving around the core Web server. From this Web location, you will discover a number of sub-communities rapidly evolving to keep up with the most of the new technologies developing in the Web and application server spaces. One of the more significant sub-communities to keep an eye on is the XML community for Apache. XML provides a common data format for evolving application servers (discussed later) into the next generation of Web services.

TUX

http://www.redhat.com/products/software/linux/tux/

TUX is a kernel-based Web server. A Web server such as Apache runs as an application on top of the Linux kernel. What makes TUX so special is the performance it can achieve as a result of being part of the kernel, as well as the integration it provides to higher level Web services. Figure 4–1 graphically shows the connection between TUX within the kernel and the Apache Web Server.

Combining TUX with the Apache Web Server is worth serious consideration for deployment within your organization.

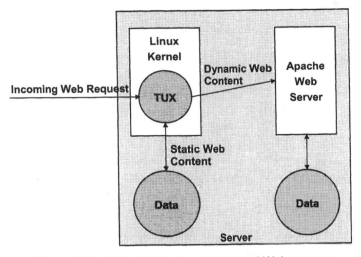

Figure 4–1 Using TUX with conventional Web servers.

JBOSS

http://www.jboss.org/

JBOSS is an open source implementation of the Java 2 Enterprise Edition (J2EE). J2EE is application server technology. Commercial implementations of J2EE include iPlanet from SUN, WebLogic from BEA, and WebSphere from IBM. Due to licensing requirements by SUN, JBOSS cannot be licensed as a certified J2EE implementation, although through work with the Apache Foundation, SUN is planning to gradually allow compliant open source implementations of J2EE. Application servers significantly enhance the capabilities of a traditional Web server. Some of these enhancements include transaction services to ensure that multiple tasks get processed as one, business logic services to allow you to build applications very quickly by combining pre-built components, and database services to allow you to access your corporate data.

As the Internet boom has progressed, much of the new application development in a number of industries is based on application server technologies. The UNIX/Linux world is often associated with Java-based application servers (J2EE), while the Windows world is associated with Microsoft's .NET (the Mono project is attempting to bring core components of the .NET framework to the open source movement). Figure 4–2 represents the connection between a Web server, application server, and database.

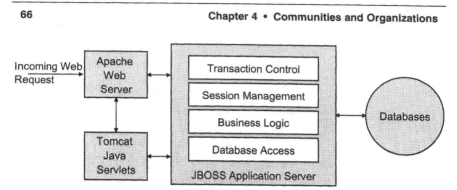

Figure 4–2   An application server connected to a Web server and database.

Depending on the sophistication of your application, open source application servers can provide a credible alternative to commercial implementations. When we look at business models in Part 3, we will take a closer look at the impact of open source on traditional business models.

Languages

A number of open source programming languages exist. Some are interpreted languages (interpreted line-by-line during execution of the program), while others are compiled (translated into machine code prior to being executed). Figure 4–3 represents the difference in how compiled and interpreted languages run on a system.

Most of the Linux kernel, device drivers, and other kernel components are written in the C programming language. However, a significant amount of software for the Web and simple scripts are based on interpreted languages such as Perl and Python. I remind you to be careful about associating these specifically to Linux. These languages and their associated interpreters/compilers are available on many other operating systems, including most flavors of UNIX as well as Windows.

GCC

http://gcc.gnu.org/

GCC is probably the most significant component that allowed Linus to develop the Linux kernel. GCC is a set of compilers used to translate higher level languages into machine code. Compiler technology is very significant in computer science since it can be the component most responsible for application performance. Compilers are typically divided

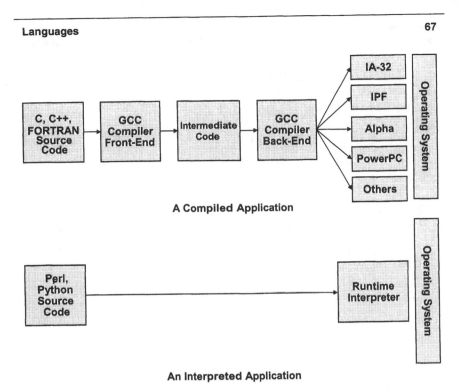

A Compiled Application

An Interpreted Application

Figure 4–3 Compiled vs. interpreted applications.

into front-end and back-end components. The front-end of a compiler translates a high-level language such as C, C++, FORTRAN, or others into an intermediate language. The back-end of a compiler does the "heavy lifting." The back-end is responsible for taking the common intermediate code and performing two primary tasks: (1) translation to machine code, and (2) optimization. The translation to machine code allows your developed application to run on the target system. It will translate in such a way that it can run on the target microprocessor architecture as well as be compatible with the operating system. Optimization techniques are the subject of advanced computer science study and application. Optimization will rearrange the code to ensure that it is run in the fastest, most efficient way possible by the target processor.

GCC is a core part of the GNU project. GCC compilers are now in wide use on a large variety of operating systems. In fact, many ISVs make the choice to do all their development using GCC to ensure maximum portability across their myriad of supported platforms.

GCC's primary design goal has been "retargetability." This means that GCC can be effectively used to target many disparate systems. However, in many cases, GCC has fallen short of performance expectations on many platforms. The result is that other companies also provide compilers that are optimized for a specific platform. If performance for your applications is paramount, then using commercial compilers available from third parties will often yield better results, but possibly at the expense of portability. If you are involved in Linux kernel development, or you want to focus on targeting as many platforms as possible, GCC is the best choice.

GCC was commercialized by Cygnus Solutions, founded by Michael Tiemann. Michael popularized one of the first open source business models. Although GCC was open source, Cygnus commercialized GCC and provided support and services for the GCC compiler base. Cygnus is now part of Red Hat.

Perl

http://www.perl.org/

Perl (Practical Extraction Report Language) is an interpreted programming language specializing in text processing. Perl has been around since 1987 with a huge following and as a result, there are a significant number of Perl experts out there. Perl is often associated with system administration, Apache, and Web applications. Since Web applications often deal with processing and manipulating text-based information, Perl provides an ideal solution. If you take a quick survey through your organization, you will likely find a few Perl developers hiding out. Since Perl is available for a wide range of operating systems, it also provides a great cross-platform solution to many development tasks.

Python

http://www.python.org/

Python is also an interpreted language. However, Python is an object-oriented language, also available for many operating system platforms. Python does not yet have the same following as Perl. But, it is a unique language that object-oriented developers, such as those familiar with C++, will learn quickly. Python is also associated with text processing, but is ideal for rapid prototyping of applications based on graphical interfaces as well. Like Perl, Python is also often used with Web applications.

Desktops and Office Productivity

One of the big differences between Linux and Windows is the availability of multiple graphical desktops instead of just the one provided by Microsoft. Some argue that this variable in the user experience creates confusion and generates additional training and support costs. Others believe that this phenomenon has created significant innovation. Both primary desktops in use with Linux are very young, with life starting near 1997. Figure 4–4 is a view of how each of the desktop environments interacts with the XFree86 core graphics library.

There have also been a number of projects aimed at providing productivity software similar to Microsoft's Office in open source form. The most popular of these is OpenOffice.

XFree86

http://www.xfree.org/

Xfree86 is the core windowing system used with all Linux systems. XFree86 is an open source implementation of the X11 framework originally developed by MIT (Massachusetts Institute of Technology). XFree86 provides the low-level connection to the graphics hardware installed on your system. If you are deploying Linux workstations or desktops, you will want to ensure that the graphics hardware installed in

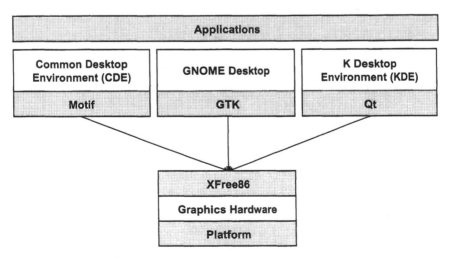

Figure 4–4   Desktop technology hierarchy.

your systems has proper support for XFree86. Although it is possible to write fully functional applications for X11, the complexity and detail required is so extensive that it is rarely done. Higher level windowing libraries that interact with X11 are most often used. For many years, the most widely used windowing library was Motif. The desktop environment used with Motif is CDE. With Linux, developers needed fully open source windowing libraries and desktop environments. This spawned two primary projects: GNOME and KDE.

GNOME

http://www.gnome.org/

The GNOME desktop is managed by the GNOME Foundation, which was set up in the late summer of 2000. GNOME is also commercialized by Ximian (formerly Helix Code) Corporation. The GNOME desktop was started by Miguel de Icaza in 1997 to provide a fully open source desktop. Each desktop is based on a core set of graphical user interface (GUI) libraries. At the time, KDE (described next) was based on a library that was not fully open source. The windowing library for writing GNOME applications is called GTK; the one for KDE is Qt. Figure 4–5 is a screen shot of the GNOME desktop.

The GNOME Foundation, which includes the likes of Ximian, Red Hat, HP, IBM, SUN Microsystems, and others guides the development of the GNOME desktop. The GNOME umbrella also includes the GNOME development platform and GNOME office.

Many UNIX vendors have also chosen the GNOME desktop as the primary desktop for their UNIX workstation environments. If you desire a consistent desktop look-and-feel between your UNIX and Linux deployments, then GNOME will generally be a good choice.

KDE

http://www.kde.org/
http://www.kdeleague.org/

KDE is also a popular desktop environment for Linux. The debate of which desktop is better is an emotional one. The reality is that it will largely boil down to a personal preference, working style, or a specific feature that may be present in one but not the other. Figure 4–6 is a screen shot of KDE in action.

Figure 4–5   The GNOME desktop.

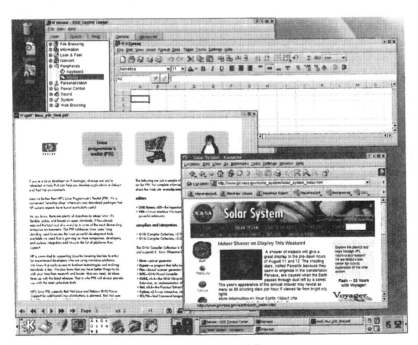

Figure 4–6   KDE.

Much like GNOME established the GNOME Foundation to bring together industry leaders to help fund and guide GNOME development, the KDE League was formed to serve a similar purpose.

Mozilla

http://www.mozilla.org/

Mozilla is an open source Web browser with a core heritage in the Netscape Web browser. Mozilla was the original code name for the Netscape product, and when Netscape made the decision to open up the Web browser, it returned to that code name. The release of Netscape is probably the most significant example of a commercial product released under an open source license. The community has learned quite a bit from the release of Mozilla. It took more than a couple of years for Mozilla to achieve the reliability and functionality that we were all accustomed to from Netscape or Microsoft's Internet Explorer.

The release of Mozilla was precipitated by the release of Internet Explorer as a no-cost addition to the Windows operating system. It was also the time that Eric Raymond released his groundbreaking paper, "The Cathedral and the Bazaar." Netscape became convinced that they could use the communal development style that Eric described in his paper to further the development of an alternative Web browser. It did not quite work out. Netscape made a few key mistakes (like releasing code that was not fully functional). Part 3 of this book is all about avoiding these and other mistakes.

Mozilla is now among the rank of credible and useful Web browsers available.

OpenOffice

http://www.openoffice.org/

Although there are a number of open source office productivity projects currently in development, OpenOffice is the one believed to present the most credible alternative to Microsoft's Office. OpenOffice is an open source implementation of the StarOffice product currently available from SUN Microsystems. SUN acquired Star Division in 2000 to provide an office productivity desktop for UNIX systems and compete directly with Microsoft. SUN provides StarOffice as a branded and supported product, while OpenOffice is a completely free system.

Databases

Databases represent the core infrastructure for many applications. They provide a number of functions for efficiently storing, organizing, and retrieving information. We normally think of databases under commercial names such as Oracle, Sybase, and DB2, among others. While these commercial implementations provide outstanding scalability, performance, and a litany of features, there are a number of cases where open source alternatives will more than meet these needs at a much lower cost.

PostgreSQL

http://www.postgresql.org/

PostgreSQL is a serious object-oriented SQL database engine. It gets its heritage from development work at UC Berkeley in the late 1970s and early 1980s. Early ancestors of PostgreSQL were released or integrated with commercial implementations from Ingres (later Computer Associates) and Informix (now IBM). With such a heritage, PostgreSQL can be taken seriously for many database applications. A number of companies also provide commercial support for PostgreSQL.

MySQL

http://www.mysql.org/

Another credible open source database alternative, MySQL, is often associated with Web applications and personal use. However, MySQL is a high-performance database with a large following, and it touts itself as the most widely used open source database.

MySQL is also another great example of dual-licensing in action. Anyone can use the MySQL database engine under the terms of the GPL. However, if you want a commercial license or you want to bundle MySQL with your product as a commercial whole, this is a great alternative.

Personal Digital Assistants

It is not possible to present an exhaustive list of all open source projects developing software for portable platforms. If you look around, you will be able to find open source applications for PalmOS, the PocketPC, and a few Linux platforms. Here are some of the core open source projects focused on Linux for handhelds.

Handheld Linux

http://www.handhelds.org/

This open source community is developing operating system and other software for handheld platforms. Most of the work today is centered on the IPAQ personal digital assistant (PDA). The community centered on this platform for development because at the time, the IPAQ stored the PocketPC OS in Flash memory. This allowed developers to overwrite the PocketPC OS with an operating system of their own. HP has also provided unofficial and casual support for the development effort.

The industry is rapidly releasing more and more PDA alternatives based on this open source development. There are even a few full-blown distributions available for handheld platforms.

Clusters

Clusters are used to horizontally scale systems for high performance, and also to provide a higher degree of availability for an entire system. There are a number of startup companies bringing support to open source clusters, or commercializing various cluster implementations. Probably the most notable Linux cluster solution for high-performance computing is the Beowulf cluster.

Beowulf

http://www.beowulf.org/

The Beowulf project represents a phenomenal example of how commodity economics affect our world of computing. The goal of the Beowulf project has been to deliver high-performance computing using commodity products. Beowulf provides a software solution to cluster a large number of nodes to provide parallel computing. If you are involved in projects that can benefit from parallel computing architectures, Beowulf is a great place to start.

Organizations

The growth and popularity of Linux and the open source movement has been helped along by a number of organizations, most of them nonprofit companies dedicated to promoting various aspects of open source development. Most of these organizations run on shoestring budgets and can use all the help they can get. Help can come in many forms such as dona-tions of equipment, resources, marketing, and, of course, cold, hard cash.

Linux International

http://www.li.org/

Linux International is the non-profit organization that promotes Linux to the world. It is run by John "Maddog" Hall. Linux International makes Linux visible to business leaders, and touts the benefits of Linux for commercial use. This group also funds projects that are of value to the Linux community as a whole.

Free Software Foundation

http://www.fsf.org/

As already mentioned, the FSF exists to promote the notion of free software for the masses. It is the brainchild of Richard Stallman, and the home of the GNU project and the GNU GPL. If you want to get a copy of the GPL text or understand the details of free software, this is the place to visit.

Open Source Initiative

http://www.opensource.org/

The OSI promotes the OSD and maintains the official list of approved open source licenses. As of this writing, there were more than 30 approved licenses. Although creating a new license is possible, you should take a detailed look at the available licenses. If you choose to release some of your software to the open source community, the odds are that there is already a license available that will meet your needs.

Open Source Development Lab

http://www.osdl.org/

The Open Source Development Lab (OSDL) was formed by a collec-tion of industry leaders motivated to promote Linux for the data center and telecommunications environments. The OSDL funds a well-equipped lab with virtually any resource someone might need to stress-test his or her open source project. Anyone can make a request to submit a project to the lab and request access to resources. The OSDL drives roadmaps of required functionality to meet the needs of these demanding environments. If you are motivated to accelerate Linux capabilities for the data center or telecommunications environments, the OSDL is a good community to get familiar with.

Free Standards Group

http://www.freestandards.org/

Chapter 7 will go into the details of standards largely promoted by the Free Standards Group (FSG). The FSG currently drives two primary working groups:

- **The Linux Standards Base (LSB)**—The LSB defines a set of interface standards to ensure portability across open source platforms.
- **Internationalization**—The Li18nux (described in Chapter 7) effort exists to drive standards to promote the use of Linux in international markets.

Embedded Linux Consortium

http://www.embedded-linux.org/

Linux for embedded applications is rapidly gaining steam and a number of Linux distributions and companies are dedicated to embedded Linux. The Embedded Linux Consortium is a trade organization dedicated to promoting Linux for embedded applications. If you are beginning an embedded project, this will provide you an excellent launch point to see if Linux will meet your needs and to find other companies you can work with.

Linux Documentation Project

http://www.linuxdoc.org/

One term that is used often in this community is "HOWTO." As the name implies, HOWTOs are simply guides that are written by anyone in the community to help with Linux tasks. There are HOWTOs available for just about any topic you can think of. The Linux Documentation Project is an effort to formalize documentation for Linux. As with everything in the open source community, anyone can contribute. The documentation project also works to provide translations to a number of the guides available.

Summary

You should come away from this chapter fully convinced that open source is not a passing fad. There are too many companies, too many groups, and too many individuals for it to go away anytime soon. The momentum is there to guarantee a bright future for a wide assortment of open source applications, and more and more of these will take a share from their commercial counterparts. If you use this class of applications in your IT environment, it is time to take a serious look. If you are a developer in any of these areas, you have new competition that does not have the same economic motivations that you do. It is time for you to learn how to take advantage of these rather than compete with them, and take your business model to a new level. Part 3 of this book will teach you how.

This chapter also represents the end of "basic training." You now have a solid grounding to learn how to deploy Linux and open source in your enterprise. Part 2 is all about taking what you have learned here and applying it to your business.

▌▌ Operational Linux

With your new core knowledge of Linux and open source, you can now dive into what it means to actually implement and deploy Linux in your business. Linux is a very large open source project. Even though this part focuses on aspects of Linux deployment, most of it is equally applicable to other open source software.

Part 2 begins with a detailed look at Linux distributions. Distributions build on the Linux kernel to give you a useful operating system. Then, we will look at the ownership impacts that Linux and open source have on your business. Next, we will take a detailed look at the standards that are relevant to Linux. Part 2 closes with the operational elements of deployment, migration, coexistence, support, and training.

CHAPTER 5

Distributions— Completing Linux

You would probably never buy just the engine of a car if you really wanted a vehicle to get from point A to point B. Downloading and building a Linux kernel would get you about as far as getting that engine. Clearly, you want a full-blown vehicle. Depending on your needs, you might choose a sedan, a wagon, a mini-van, or any of a myriad of vehicles. Even when you know what you want, you might select a number of different features.

Think of a Linux distribution in much the same way. Distributions combine the Linux kernel with a host of other capabilities to make sure you can run your business. Some will specialize in broad market applications, while others will focus on specific niches, while still others will focus on geographic segments. Understanding the details of how a distribution comes together is a key part of understanding Linux. In this chapter, you will learn:

- What a distribution is
- Packages and dependencies
- Who are the major distribution vendors
- What makes one distribution different from another
- What you should consider when selecting a distribution
- Distribution dependencies
- A cursory view of standards related to distributions

Linux distributions represent what you will acquire and deploy within your company. If you build applications, understanding the difference between distributions will ensure that you can support as many environments as possible.

Linux Distribution

When most people refer to "Linux," they are generally referring to a Linux distribution. As you will soon learn, a distribution is assembled by any number of vendors and combines many components over and above the kernel. Distribution vendors generally perform the following tasks:

- Select a specific kernel version
- Create or select patches to add new functionality or solve known problems
- Select the specific collection of packages and their versions
- Add their own value-added enhancements such as installation and deployment tools
- Combine the entire collection on distribution media
- Certify and test each component, as well as the whole distribution
- In some cases, bundle in third-party applications or features
- Apply their individual brand image
- Select go-to-market channels for distribution
- Offer value-added services in conjunction with the distribution

Every Linux distribution is different, sometimes subtly, sometimes blatantly. However, Figure 5–1 gives you a view of the structure common to almost all distributions. As you can see, the distribution includes far more than just the kernel.

Distribution vendors perform significant amounts of work to bring Linux to you. How well they do this work and how well they support their work will be prime factors in choosing a distribution to install.

Most distribution vendors combine a collection of packages (discussed next) that are all open source. This implies that their distribution can be downloaded and copied at no cost. Therefore, distribution vendors have been evolving their business models in order to sustain their growth. Here is a quick summary of how most distribution vendors make their money:

- Selling boxed sets with media and documentation through retail channels
- Providing support and update services

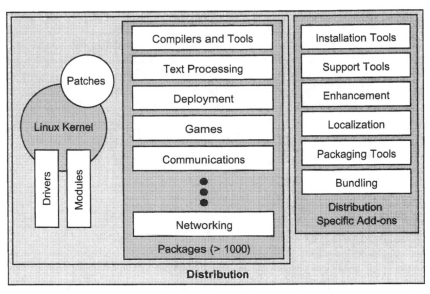

Figure 5–1 Generic view of a Linux distribution.

- Delivering professional services specific to their Linux distribution
- Collecting original equipment manufacturer (OEM) fees for those who bundle the distribution with their hardware or software product

Distribution vendors continue to evolve their business models and this list will inevitably expand. In Part 3, I will go into the details of Linux and open source business models.

Packages

Every distribution has the notion of a "package," where the distribution is the sum of all the packages available for a given release. Each package in turn consists of one or more files that, in general, implement a single function (e.g., a compiler, a browser, a Web server, etc.). But, to be clear, it is the package maintainer that decides the granularity of a package. Some packages will be large and contain thousands of files, while others will be very small and contain only a file or two. Figure 5–2 depicts the typical layout of a package. As you can see, a package contains both the files needed to make any given function work, as well as the information needed by the package manager to install the package on the target system.

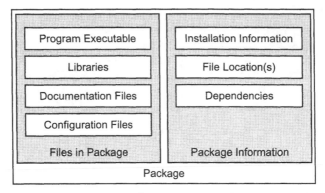

Figure 5–2   Generic package layout.

The list in Table 5–1 is taken from the Debian stable package listing; other distribution vendors may categorize their lists differently. Obviously, I can't list all of the packages here (there are almost 9000 available just for Debian), but the table lists the major package categories.

Table 5–1   Package Categories

Package Category	Description
Administration Utilities	Utilities to administer system resources, manage user accounts, and perform other similar administrative tasks.
Communication Programs	Software to communicate using a traditional modem.
Development	Development utilities, compilers, development environments, and libraries.
Documentation	Frequently asked questions (FAQs), HOWTO guides, and other documents.
Editors	Software to edit files usually associated with programming environments.
Electronics	Electronics utilities.
Games	Entertainment.
Graphics	Editors, viewers, and converters.
Ham Radio	Software for Ham radio.
Interpreters	All kinds of interpreters for interpreted languages and macro processors.

(continued)

Package Category	Description
Libraries	Libraries to make other programs work. They provide special features to developers.
Mail	Programs to route, read, and compose email messages.
Mathematics	Math software.
Miscellaneous	Miscellaneous utilities that don't fit well anywhere else.
Network	Daemons (background processes) and clients to connect Linux to the world.
Newsgroups	Software to access Usenet and set up news servers.
Software Restricted by Law or Patent	Most of these packages can be used in the U.S., but they can't be exported (not even re-exported!).Some of these packages may not be used in the U.S. or other countries due to patents. You should carefully review the restrictions on the use of such packages and consult with your attorney if you have questions.
Old Libraries	Old versions of libraries, kept for backward compatibility with old applications.
Other Operating Systems and File Systems	Software to run programs compiled for other operating systems, and to use their file systems.
Shells	Command shells. Friendly user interfaces for beginners.
Sound	Utilities to deal with sound: mixers, players, recorders, and CD players.
TeX	The famous typesetting software and related programs.
Text Processing	Utilities to format and print text documents.
Utilities	Utilities for file/disk manipulation, backup and archive tools, system monitoring, and input systems.
Web Software	Web servers, browsers, proxies, and download tools.
X Window System Software	X servers, libraries, fonts, window managers, terminal emulators, and many related applications.

Each package has a maintainer or group of maintainers. Also, each package will have a number of different versions available. In many cases, these packages can be found localized for any number of languages. Distribution vendors make a selection of not only which packages to include with their distribution, they also decide which version, with what patches, and which local languages to support.

For a distribution vendor to include a package in a distribution, the package must support the kernel version being included, there must be a version available for the processor being supported, and the chosen language must be supported. There may be other dependencies (on other packages, for example), but these are the core requirements. The Venn diagram in Figure 5–3 demonstrates the conditions that need to be met for a package to be included in a distribution.

You must always remember that one of the key contributions that open source represents is that you are in control, *not* your vendors. If you don't like any of the decisions that your distribution provider has made, you can make as many changes as you like. If you would like a particular package that has not been included, you can usually find it on the Internet and download a copy for installation.

Package Formats

Packages are combined and built from files through the use of special tools that generate a special module ready for deployment. There are two popular package formats: One was developed by Red Hat and is called the Red Hat Package Manager, or RPM; the other comes from the Debian community and is referred to as the DEB (or "dot-deb") package format.

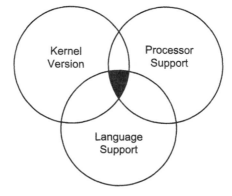

Figure 5–3   Package inclusion Venn diagram.

Distribution Vendors

There are far too many distribution vendors to list them all here. If you count all the specialized distributions and distributions of local interest, they number well into the hundreds. I will focus on some of the distributions in the mainstream (those with significant brand awareness or market share) as well as examples of a few distributions focused on specific target markets or geographies. You can find a more complete listing of distributions at the *Linux.org* Web site.

Mainstream Distributions

Red Hat

In many corners of the world, Red Hat is the most widely recognized Linux distribution. Red Hat is also one of the few publicly traded companies focused completely on Linux. Bob Young and Marc Ewing formed Red Hat in 1994. It was one of the first examples of making Linux easy to use and install. Red Hat commands an impressive market share, but does not dominate in all parts of the world.

Red Hat uses its distribution as an effective calling card, espousing its heritage and commitment to Linux. They employ a number of developers that directly contribute to the Linux kernel and other parts of the operating system. They have made innovations in a number of areas such as the RPM.

When we examine business models in more detail, you will see that Red Hat has focused much of its energy in developing its support and services business. They determined early on that selling licenses for free software was likely not going to be a sustainable business for them. However, Red Hat has remained true to open source. They have refused to bundle or ship any software that does not strictly meet the definition of open source. This may or may not be sustainable, and only time will tell.

Recall also that Red Hat acquired Cygnus Solutions, which gave them the key role as maintainers of the GCC compiler tool suite.

The combination of one of the most popular Linux distributions, plus an array of support and services offerings, makes Red Hat a truly credible player in the Linux space.

SuSE

Based in Germany, SuSE offers an impressive distribution that can be used on a wide variety of microprocessor architectures. Due to its base in Germany, SuSE is also a favorite in the European region. SuSE has often been called the technology leader for Linux. This distribution can be used in both client and server environments, and is also used by a number of ISVs as their core development platform. Often considered the most viable contender to Red Hat, some aspects of SuSE's business model are very similar to Red Hat, while other aspects are quite different. SuSE's business model has evolved differently with a focus on supporting multiple platforms as well as bundling and reselling third-party software with Linux. This gives them a revenue stream tied to OEM vendors and software licenses.

Caldera

Caldera has had an interesting evolution in the world of Linux. Once dedicated to Linux, Caldera's acquisition of SCO has given it the ability to draw on an impressive installed base. Caldera has now both Linux and UNIX products and focuses on some of the key integration between the two offerings. Caldera has also been developing value-added products to give it the ability to charge license revenues in addition to the support and professional services it offers.

TurboLinux

TurboLinux has had its strongest showing in Asian markets. Although Red Hat has been encroaching on this TurboLinux stronghold, TurboLinux is still very strong in this market. One of the key enhancements that TurboLinux ships with its distribution is an Asian language extension, which is why it has been a favorite. TurboLinux has attempted a number of different business model options, including a failed merger attempt with LinuxCare, a firm dedicated to cross-vendor Linux support services.

TurboLinux now has a business model·focused on delivering solutions for manageability, clustering, and databases, as well as providing its distribution for a number of different microprocessor platforms.

Mandrake

Mandrake started life as "a better Red Hat." Mandrake took the original Red Hat base and added a number of usability enhancements as well as a distribution compiled and optimized for the latest generation of Intel processors. Over time, Mandrake has distanced itself from Red Hat. It continues its strong showing as a desktop Linux and attempts to expand as a credible offering for server systems. Mandrake is based in France, which also makes it another favorite among Europeans, second only to Red Hat.

Debian

Debian is an interesting distribution since it has no commercial connections. It is the only mainstream distribution that is 100% community-driven. Ian Murdock founded Debian. The name Debian is the merge of his wife's name, Debby, and his name, Ian.

This disconnection from a corporate identity makes Debian a favorite among community leaders and developers. The Debian community includes hundreds of developers and much of their work will find its way into the other mainstream distributions. Also, remember that the OSD takes its heritage from the Debian Social Contract (*www.debian.org/social_contract*).

Debian probably boasts the most supported platforms of any distribution. Many companies contribute to Debian since no corporate agenda drives the development and contributions are readily accepted. Since everything is always open, competitors can operate on an even playing field. If you are a software vendor and need to standardize components specific to your industry, Debian may be the best environment for you to work in.

Many community groups and organizations use Debian as a base for their work, then provide support for other distributions from there. Debian has been criticized for lagging the other distributions in supporting the latest innovation in packages and kernel releases. But, this really is a double-edged sword. While Debian may track somewhat behind the other distributions, it is widely recognized as having some of the most comprehensive integration testing across the broadest range of platforms, and the most stable release of any.

For enterprises looking for the most open distribution with total vendor independence that will offer some impressive stability, Debian can be a good choice. The primary downside is that due to the lack of corporate backing, Debian is often the last choice for commercial application developers.

United Linux

United Linux (UL) is a joining of many leading Linux distribution vendors to create one single Linux Standards Base-, or LSB-compliant Linux distribution (discussed in Chapter 7). Since creating a distribution is an expensive proposition and it is difficult for vendors to differentiate their offerings, many vendors have joined together to create one single Linux distribution. By combining their efforts they can share the costs of creating the base distribution and focus their efforts on more concrete and customer visible value.

At the time of this writing, the UL initiative was just getting started. It is too soon to tell if the UL will gain traction in the industry as a common distribution. The good news is that the effort is also ensuring LSB conformance to enable application compatibility.

Geographic Distributions

Some distributions respond to the specific needs of local markets. As examples, I have outlined a few here, but this is not meant to be a comprehensive list. Depending on where you live, there may be a local distribution that will meet your needs.

Red Flag

Red Flag Linux strives to bring the Linux operating system to greater China. Red Flag provides both mainstream and embedded Linux distributions. Enhancements to Red Flag Linux are focused on localization for the Asian market.

If you are the provider of Linux applications and you decide to target China with your products, then establishing a partnership with a local provider such as Red Flag should be considered a business imperative.

Connectiva

Distinguished as a Latin American-based distribution, Connectiva is based in Brazil and distributes Linux in Spanish and Portuguese. Connectiva also provides a number of services and training (like most other distribution providers), focused on businesses in the Latin American market.

Specialty Distributions

The following examples demonstrate how certain distribution providers focus on specific niche markets. In most cases, these providers are highly specialized in a specific field of interest.

MSC.Linux

MSC.Software specializes in high-performance computing applications and is well-known in its field. MSC creates a distribution focused on the high-performance, simulation, and clustering market. MSC combines its specialized distribution with hardware, consulting, and customization to give their customers a fully working system optimized for their specific application environment.

MontaVista

MontaVista (their distribution originally had a brand name of Hard Hat Linux) is focused on the embedded and telecommunications Linux markets and provides a distribution focused on applications that require support for small, embedded processors. They also provide enhanced kernel features to provide real-time capabilities. MontaVista supports a number of embedded processor types, provides a development environment focused on embedded applications, and takes care to support specialized computer board types (cPCI, VME, and others).

Non-Linux Operating System Distributions

The term "distribution" is also used to refer to any packaging of files, programs, tools, and utilities, but is not the Linux operating system. One of the best examples of this is the GNOME desktop distribution. While a Linux distribution may include a set of packages that installs a GNOME desktop, commercial vendors may create enhanced and branded package collections that will be referred to as a "GNOME distribution."

Continuing our example of the GNOME desktop, Ximian creates a distribution that combines:

- The packages required to run GNOME
- Developer tools and enhancements
- Source code
- Office productivity software
- Software update capabilities
- Versions for different operating systems (e.g., HP-UX, Solaris)
- Media and documentation

This represents but one example. A number of commercial companies have attempted to create distributions for any number of subcomponents of the Linux operating system. Some attempts have been more successful than others. The key point for you to remember is that while the term "distribution" is most often tied to Linux, there are cases where it will be applied to other application collections.

Creating Your Own Distribution

Many enterprises will find that they need to create a customized distribution to support the special needs of their organization. However, the process of creating your own distribution should not be taken lightly. Depending on how extensive your changes are, and how customized your distribution is, you can incur significant costs. Typically, enterprise-class, customized distributions are set up with:

- A specific Linux kernel with predetermined patches and modules
- Corporate branding elements
- Special deployment tools and capabilities specific to your corporation
- Preconfigured management agents
- Pre-installed applications licensed for the organization
- Preconfigured network and other components
- Security setup according to company standards
- Special capabilities for interoperability with the rest of the enterprise
- Support for specific hardware used in the corporation
- Removal of all nonessential packages
- A kernel and packages compiled and optimized for specific hardware configurations
- A number of distribution setups for the various environments deployed throughout the organization (desktop, server, multi-processor server, etc.)

Creating your own distribution should only be done when your IT organization has developed enough core competence to manage the ongoing changes to all of the packages that will make up your distribution. "Rolling-your-own" should be treated as any other significant software project undertaken by your IT organization. Figure 5–4 demonstrates two typical flowcharts used to create a custom distribution.

The process on the left starts with a mainstream distribution and strips away unwanted components, then adds new ones. The process on the right starts from a raw Linux kernel and builds up from there. Which process you select will depend on your specific needs and the degree of control and customization you desire.

Supporting Multiple Distributions

For large multinational companies, one of the key choices will be to decide if your company will support a single distribution for all deployments, or if multiple distributions will be qualified for various application or geographic deployments.

As a software vendor, you would like to maximize your addressable market. When you first decide to make your applications available on Linux, you may be tempted to just pick the one that is most familiar to you. Eventually, one of your customers will require you to support an

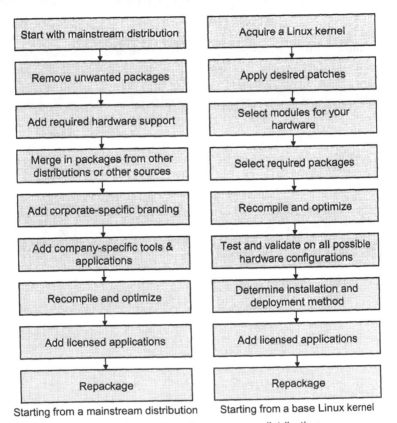

Starting from a mainstream distribution   Starting from a base Linux kernel

Figure 5–4   Creating your own distribution.

alternate distribution, or even a custom in-house distribution. Standards are being developed to ensure that differences between distributions don't have a negative impact on software vendors. You should do all you can to follow those standards, and because of their critical nature, I will cover them extensively in Chapter 7.

The other technique used by software vendors (or IT shops developing in-house applications) is to focus on component dependencies rather than distributions. Develop a list of dependencies such as:

- Kernel version
- Required patches
- Required packages
- All package versions
- External application dependencies
- Hardware requirements

This comprehensive list will remove the base distribution dependency and rapidly allow you to support any distribution that your market demands. This does not remove the need to test your applications with specific distribution and hardware combinations, but it ensures that you are not developing undesired dependencies into a specific distribution that will limit your future market opportunities.

Standards

Chapter 7 will take a detailed look at standards related to Linux and distributions. In general, all distributions are based on a common kernel and a common set of packages. However, each distribution will make different choices for versions of these components and may also make different choices on what to include and exclude. If you decide to run Linux on non-mainstream microprocessor architectures, you may also have fewer packages than Linux installed on mainstream systems.

There are a number of standards being developed to ensure that distributions can create value, while ensuring that application and hardware vendors can easily support all distributions equally.

Summary

You should now have a clear understanding of what choice points are available to you in selecting what you will likely deploy in your environment. Distributions are a collection of packages brought together and tested to make sure the collection of versions all work together. Distributions allow you to install and deploy a sensible collection of software to operate your business.

In the next chapter, we will look at the cost of Linux. While you can acquire distributions for little to no cost, an effective deployment and support of the environment will cost you over the life of the system. However, how you measure these costs may be considerably different than what you calculated in the past.

The Cost of Linux
and Open Source

*L*inux is free! Well, not exactly. Any seasoned manager clearly understands that component costs represent a small portion of the big picture and that the whole solution, over a lifetime, must be considered. The industry term is "total cost of ownership," or TCO. Remember that car from the previous chapter that will now get you from point A to point B? Depending on the car, you will need to consider the cost of gas, insurance, maintenance, parts, and a number of other factors over the lifetime of your vehicle. Technology acquisitions, including open source, are no different—especially for open source, due to the perception that "free" implies "without cost."

In this chapter we will examine the cost elements associated with open source that might be different from any other cost calculations you might have done in the past. Remember that Linux is simply a very large open source project. Although you may have a tendency to focus on the cost of Linux, virtually everything I outline can be applied to any open source application you choose to deploy. The goals for this chapter are:

- Understanding the total cost of a solution
- The effects of open source on solutions costs
- How to procure open source software
- Which business processes need to be reexamined

This will give you the information you need to consider the total cost associated with deploying and running a Linux environment.

The Costs

Linux and other open source software radically alter how you measure the cost of a solution. Here are some of the traditional costs associated with an Information Technology based solution:

- Hardware
- Operating system
- Networking infrastructure
- Administration tools and utilities
- Deployment
- Upgrades to the solutions in use
- Ongoing management and administration, including license-tracking
- Environmental (floor space, power, air conditioning, etc.)
- Application licenses
- Support fees (for all components)
- Unplanned downtime
- Extended warranties
- Training
- Disasters and other business risks

When doing cost calculations to measure a return on investment (ROI), you will also clearly identify the initial acquisition costs and ongoing maintenance costs. For example, the cost of buying the initial license for a new application can be very small when compared to the support costs of that application over its lifetime. Vendors will often bundle some of these component costs (e.g., hardware with operating system), making calculations and comparisons a difficult task. Figure 6–1 is a theoretical representation of the relative costs of deploying computer solutions in a typical enterprise.

Since every enterprise is different, Figure 6–1 only attempts to show a typical cost calculation scenario (your environment could be substantially different). The chart shows relative (and typical) percentages for the costs of deploying a complete solution. The bar chart shows a relative percentage between the initial cost of acquiring that component of

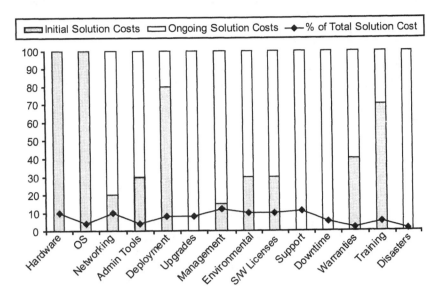

Figure 6–1 Sample cost profile for implementing a computer solution (S/W stands for software).

a solution and the ongoing costs of keeping the solution going. For example, the environmental costs include some initial costs (building a computer room, installing air and power, etc.), but there are also ongoing environmental costs associated with maintaining the environment. The gray part of the bar shows the initial fixed cost; the white part of the bar shows the ongoing costs. The line chart shows a typical relative percentage for each component as part of the total solution.

What you can see is that most components have fixed costs and variable, ongoing costs. In most cases, the ongoing costs represent a larger percentage than the fixed costs. We also see that no one component represents a huge part of the overall solution. The complexity not demonstrated here is that most enterprises will deploy multiple solutions, and that many of the component costs can and will be aggregated across solution deployments. Your business analysis will need to take that complexity into account. The key factor is that if you are deploying multiple solutions, and you can aggregate your fixed costs, then the components touched by open source will have a much greater impact on potential cost savings.

The Open Source Effect

Since understanding the costs is probably one of the most important aspects to consider in deploying Linux and open source software, it is worth going through each of the elements of the list that benefit or suffer from the effect of open source. Some of the elements on this list are covered in greater detail in later chapters.

Hardware

Open source software affects hardware costs in a couple of different ways. This is also where the specifics of the Linux operating system play a key role. As I mentioned in Chapters 1 and 2, virtually all open source software, including Linux, is developed on open commodity computing. Since there is no need to depend on proprietary hardware solutions, the cost of hardware can be reduced considerably. This assumes that the combination of an open platform with Linux will meet your scalability, reliability, availability, and performance needs. Another consideration is the hardware ecosystem available as a result of using an open platform. This means that there is generally a huge selection of supported hardware add-ons available. This selection increases your solution options, and the competitive effect will also reduce your costs.

Many users have also reported that the combination of Linux and open source software will run on much older hardware configurations than proprietary solutions. Linux is often deployed on much older hardware as a reuse option. Also, low-performance hardware solutions can often meet your business' needs for a much lower cost. Finally, some will choose to re-use proprietary hardware, or use a portion of an existing system to take advantage of the benefits of Linux.

Operating System

Proprietary operating systems can cost well into the hundreds of thousands of dollars on large systems. Linux can be acquired, replicated, and installed with no associated license costs. Probably more significant is the ongoing support, upgrade, and maintenance costs associated with the operating system over the life of the system. I will cover this in more detail later. Obviously, there is an expectation that the hardware and operating system combination meets your business needs.

As I outlined in Chapter 5, you have the ability to combine a number of different components to build your own Linux distribution. Rather than needing to acquire component parts, you can assemble open source parts into your own operating system.

Depending on your application and the size of your organization, modifying commercial Linux distributions for your particular needs can inject new costs in the form of self-maintenance or custom support contracts.

Administration Tools and Utilities

Almost any large corporation has developed a significant suite of tools that are specific to the organization. Oftentimes, these tools were developed years ago, and the original developer has long left the company. In some cases, the source code for these internal tools and utilities is nowhere to be found. Your costs of maintaining and migrating these internal tools to other platforms can be very substantial.

This is the open source "sweet spot." In many cases, almost any function you can think of has been written by another developer in the community. If it is not available, then there will usually be something close that can be leveraged and adapted to your needs. The wonderful part of this is that your extensions to any tool can be contributed back to the community and maintained on an ongoing basis by the community. This presents a significant opportunity for reducing your costs. Contributions to the community will build goodwill and a real desire on the part of the community to help you in return.

Upgrades to the Solution

Upgrades to your deployment are always done on *your terms* and on *your schedule.* You never need to be concerned about the loss of vendor support. Since the source code is always available, you can always choose to support your own environment. In the case of large open source projects such as Linux and Apache, you will have the choice of several companies from which to obtain support or you can support yourself with backup from the community.

The other factor is the cost of license fees associated with upgrades. Many software vendors charge maintenance fees to get minor updates to their software, and significant new license charges for upgrades to major new releases. With open source software, these ongoing costs vanish.

Management, Administration, and License-Tracking

When I discuss deployment in more detail in Chapter 8, you will understand that one of the considerations for deploying a Linux environment is the ability to integrate it into your existing infrastructure.

Large corporations usually spend millions of dollars every year just to track software licenses. Many companies develop sophisticated tools to track licenses on a global basis, while others do everything possible to negotiate corporate licenses with vendors in an effort to reduce tracking costs. With open source software distributed under an OSI-approved license, there is no need to track licenses and it is perfectly legal to replicate as many copies of the software as you need.

Application and Other Software Licenses

The most obvious place you can reduce costs is by eliminating the cost of licensing software. For many, this is still a new concept. In many cases, you actually buy open source software—you might have seen boxed sets of your favorite Linux distribution at your local electronics store. The big difference is that you are not buying a license to the software. In the case of open source software, you are buying convenience and a brand you trust. In most cases, this takes the form of media (the CD/DVD to load the software), documentation, and in many cases, some form of support from the company offering the bundle.

When we go through support in more detail, you will see the options available to you. For now, be aware that there is no requirement to pay license fees on open source software. You can usually download the software from any number of locations, create your own CDs, and even print your own documentation. You have to decide how much convenience you are willing to pay for.

Support Fees

One of the most common business models associated with open source is to offer support. When you deal with proprietary software, your support options are significantly limited. You can usually only get support from the vendor selling the software. As a result of a captive audience, the vendor can charge a premium for support services.

Even if your plan is to treat open source software in much the same way as commercial software, the simple fact that support services will be available from multiple vendors increases competition and has a positive effect on price. Operationally, you need to alter your business processes to look at support as a competitive bidding process.

Unplanned Downtime

In the world of proprietary software, some defects can cause unexpected and undesirable downtime. For mission-critical environments, you will often negotiate very extensive support arrangements to minimize these scenarios. However, the fact remains that you are at the mercy of your vendor. If your vendor does not want to make the changes needed, in the timeframe you need, you will often be left with very little recourse.

Again, even in an environment where you choose to work with open source software as if it were commercial software, the fundamental ability to work with the community at large or your own internal expert IT staff to fix problems that arise can reduce the cost of unplanned downtime.

Training

As I mentioned in Chapter 1, the availability of trained resources is one of the key benefits of Linux moving forward. If you deploy an industry standard, open environment, then your training costs should be reduced by the simple fact that trained resources are available. However, if you are migrating from an existing environment, then training costs could represent a substantial investment that you need to consider.

Regardless of the type of deployment you have, open source software requires a different set of behaviors from developers, purchasing officers, contract negotiators, and the management team. This book is giving you the details you need to understand how those behaviors are different, but you need to consider the associated costs.

Adapting to an Imperfect Solution

In the early days of computing, most environments were custom-built from the ground up. As a result, the solution came very close to meeting your needs perfectly. However, developing these solutions was a very expensive proposition. Over time, software vendors built generic applications that could be applied to a wide range of problems. Although the solution was not perfect, the costs were so dramatically lower that it was worth the tradeoff of an imperfect solution. However, this is a cost to consider in your business, and a very unique benefit of open source that is often overlooked.

This is where open source can shine. The ability to procure open source software that approximates your business needs and then customize it to your specific needs allows you to have the best of both worlds. As I mentioned earlier, in many cases, the open source community will welcome many of your enhancements, accept them into the core source tree, and support the complete environment.

Measuring this benefit can be complex, since you must analyze and compare where costs no longer exist, plus account for incremental costs. With this analysis, you can construct a business case. Table 6–1 gives you a guide to do this analysis:

Table 6–1   Implementing a "Perfect" Solution

Eliminated and Reduced Costs	New or Increased Costs	Zero Costs
Software license fees for the "imperfect" solution	Adapting the open source solution to the business-specific needs	Accept open source software solution
Extra personnel to maintain the imperfect solution	Maintenance and support of any components rejected by the community	Accept community efforts to integrate customization
Implemented workarounds	Personnel to influence and maintain contact with community developments	Ongoing updates provided by the community
Customization	Expert personnel	Start from the existing published code base
Other business impacts (e.g., time to market, customer satisfaction, etc.)		More extensive community-based quality assurance

Obviously this table of cost comparisons needs to be combined with all of the other cost factors outlined in this chapter. The point here is that open source offers you an opportunity to achieve a near perfect solution at a reasonable cost. Your own individual business analysis will determine if the new solution is worth it.

Procuring Linux and Open Source Software

When acquiring traditional software products, your company will likely have established a comprehensive process with vendors and suppliers. You negotiate license fees based on volume and you choose from a few select suppliers, or even a single supplier, to keep your overall costs to a minimum. Whether you acquire Linux, Apache, or any other open source software, the processes for acquisition are radically different. Consider the example of procuring the Linux operating system. Here are the most common ways to get a copy of Linux:

- Purchase a boxed set from a local supplier
- Download CD images from the Internet
- Use a CD included with a book or bundled with another product
- Use software preloaded or bundled with a computer system or peripheral

There are similar ways to acquire virtually any open source software. In some cases, software vendors will include open source utilities, tools, and add-on applications with their own software.

Purchasing agents in your organization will likely be trained to acquire and account for licenses for any software that is purchased. Left unchecked, it may be equally likely that they will be tempted to apply these same processes to open source software. However, it is important that your teams be trained to only purchase open source software that includes elements your business believes is worth paying for (manuals, media, support, etc.).

In the case where hardware or software vendors bundle branded open source software, you should be aware that you may be paying additional fees for the bundling. Branded open source software usually refers to a marketing arrangement between two companies that allows the use of brand and trademark associations between the companies. In many instances, the hardware and software vendors will be bundling open source components that may be available elsewhere at no cost. However, there may be cases where the convenience of bundling is worth an additional cost to you. The point is for you to be aware of what you are getting for your money. It is always possible for you to acquire open source software from another source, or to replicate as many copies as you need within your organization. There is no need to track licenses in use.

Contracts

If you are a software or hardware vendor, it is typical to require indemnification from any vendor whose software you incorporate, or bundle with your own. When it comes to open source software, the rules change. Since most open source software is written by a collection of individuals, and there can be literally hundreds of different copyright owners, no one can afford to give you such indemnification.

Remember, in any contract negotiation with a commercial vendor that packages open source software, you are not negotiating simply for the cost of a software license. You are likely negotiating for support, services, and specialized consulting. Also remember that this is a competitive environment, and you will have many options available to you.

Modifying Open Source Software

Many industry analysts recommend against modifying open source software, and recommend that you treat it as any other proprietary software within your corporation. This recommendation comes from the fact that changing the software for your specific uses will imply picking up the support burden for the new software solution. For smaller companies with a small IT staff, this can in fact be an appropriate answer. However, for large corporations that can engage with the open source community, the ability to modify the software can be a great opportunity to reduce costs. Modifying open source software should always be done with a view to contributing the changes back to the maintainers within the community.

This ability to modify open source software brings a number of benefits to both large corporations and ISVs:

• Influence the direction of the software product
• Invest in making your priorities real, on your schedule
• Getting an inside view to help future planning

You should note that the maintainer is in control. Influence is based on sustained participation. When analyzing the costs of Linux and open source, consider the costs of waiting for a vendor to make your priorities real, compared to the costs of making direct investments and contributing to make your priorities real.

If you are unwilling or unable to join the community and participate in the future of any software product, then the analysts are absolutely right. You should stay away from making any modifications to open source software and only use it when it has been packaged and is supported by a commercial vendor.

Summary

You should now be able to see how Linux and open source affect the costs of a solution throughout your business. In most cases, you can reap tremendous benefits and significantly lower the costs in your environment. However, you also learned that open source does not directly translate into zero costs. There are no license fees associated with open source software and there is no requirement for you to pay for open source software, even if it has been bundled with other components, but you may have to pick up the costs to maintain the solution yourself. Your procurement and contract negotiation processes may need to be revised. Finally, you can control your costs further by making clear decisions to modify software, return it to the community, and reap the benefits of a solution that most closely matches your business needs.

One of the key elements in keeping costs low throughout the ecosystem is standards. The next chapter will examine the standards that are specific to the Linux environment. Promoting these standards will encourage the growth of the ecosystem and keep the costs low by ensuring that choice and competition continue to be available.

Standards—One Linux

*Y*ou have now built your car, starting at the engine, and then combined it with all the options you want. You have a clear view of what your car is going to cost you through the life of the vehicle. But now imagine if everyone's car was built with enough differences that you couldn't share the same roads and highways, or if every car used a completely different kind of fuel. The odds are pretty good that we would not have our network of roads and highways, and that driving a vehicle would be restricted to a few select individuals. While it is important that every car manufacturer can build vehicles with unique characteristics to meet the various needs of different customers, it is equally important that there be a common set of standards that allow everyone to benefit from this form of transportation.

In this chapter, we will go through the details of standards specific to Linux and open source software currently available and under development. Only standards that are new and specific to Linux will be discussed here. Also, this chapter focuses on the aspects of standards that ensure application portability. Therefore, the goals for this chapter are to understand:

- Why Linux and open source standards are needed
- The key standards and how they work
- Conformance and testing
- Where the standards don't apply

This will give you the information you need to successfully focus on the right set of standards to ensure that you will continue to maintain all of the benefits of an open environment.

Why Standards?

Based on your knowledge from previous chapters, you know that a Linux distribution is a combination of the Linux kernel, modules, patches, the suite of GNU system tools, and host of other add-ons. Distribution vendors need to be commended for their work in packaging Linux in such as way that it has become relatively easy to install and deploy. But, this entrepreneurial spirit and the desire to innovate created a world where differences between each distribution benefited almost no one. Here are some of the key examples of different choices distribution vendors make:

- Kernel version
- Integrated patches
- Modules, drivers, and versions
- Location of files
- Package versions

Almost everyone in the Linux industry (end-users, distribution vendors, and application vendors) has come to realize that these differences are having the simple and undesired effect of slowing Linux adoption. As a result, the top distribution vendors, as well as the hardware vendors, ISVs, and notable open source developers such as Linus himself, have grouped together to create a set of standards managed by the Free Standards Group. It is obviously important for there to be significant benefits to creating new standards. Before we look at the details of the standards under the Free Standards Group here are the key advantages and winners behind these standard efforts:

- **End-users**—The final end-user will often be medium to large corporations with a presence all over the world. Linux standards allow end-users to select distributions of local interest while ensuring that they have one support model for the entire enterprise. End-users also benefit by ensuring maximum application support on their platform of choice.

- **Distribution vendors**—The investment to create a distribution is not insignificant. The more standards there are, the more leverage there can be between each of the distributions, thereby reducing the investment. Also, standards have clearly demonstrated the effect of making the market much larger. Consider the Internet. Had we not had standards, the size of the Internet would be substantially reduced, and we likely would not have had the industry transformation that took place in the late 1990s. Distribution vendors win in two primary areas: 1) maintaining compatibility between versions; 2) a clear definition of where the "universal" commonality layer ends and the "unique" value-added begins.
- **Software vendors**—Creating applications for multiple variants of UNIX has already demonstrated an expensive history. Software vendors will typically be forced to make a tradeoff between the cost of supporting many versions of their application and the size of the available market. Standards allow software vendors to create one version of their software and support it on the broadest set of platforms.

Linux and open source software have now matured to the point where the only way to assure sustainable growth of the industry is to have standards that will ensure a focus on new innovation rather than on managing differences that add no value.

Free Standards Group

The Free Standards Group (*www.freestandards.org*) is a non-profit organization whose primary mission in life is to grow the use and acceptance of open source technologies through standards. The natural outcome of their work will move Linux to the next stage of market growth: an enterprise platform for commercial applications. The Free Standards Group's three primary workgroups are:

- **The Linux Standards Base (LSB)**—The LSB is a set of interface standards and test suites allowing for ultimate portability of applications across Linux, allowing an application to run regardless of distribution or version number.
- **The Linux Internationalization Initiative (Li18nux)**—This standard creates a foundation for language and cultural localization of compliant distribution and applications.

- **The File System Hierarchy (FSH) standard**—This standard ensures a consistent model for file locations on UNIX, and now Linux systems. This is one of the key standards on which the LSB depends. The FSH standard is discussed with the LSB.

The Free Standards Group does not attempt to do all the standards work on its own and is also affiliated with another standards initiative relevant to Linux: the X Desktop Group. The X Desktop Group is focused on standards to encourage cooperation and interoperability between UNIX and Linux desktops. You have already learned about the two major desktops on Linux: GNOME and KDE. The Free Standards Group also works very closely with the XFree86 group (recall Chapter 4) and continues to be interested in expanding the standards into the user interface arena.

As a non-profit corporation, the Free Standards Group is funded by major industry vendors who obviously understand the significant benefits brought about by these standards. Any end-user, ISV, or hardware vendor is encouraged to participate. Standards are only successful when they meet the requirements of those who use them and when they reflect broad involvement in the community. The more the merrier.

Linux Standards Base

The LSB (www.linuxbase.org) is the core standard that ensures a successful marriage between Linux distributions and Linux applications. Specifically, it is a:

- Binary interface specification (a binary specification implies that applications do not need to be recompiled when moving from system to system) that ensures application compatibility across all certified Linux distributions.
- Set of test suites to test both Linux distributions and Linux-based applications for LSB conformance.
- Build environment to develop LSB-compliant applications.
- Sample implementation to run and test applications in a "pure" LSB environment.

By utilizing the standards and tools, distribution vendors create LSB-conforming Linux distributions, and application vendors create LSB-conforming software applications.

By focusing on a common set of interfaces, an application vendor can write and test an application according to the LSB and be assured that the application will run on any LSB-compliant distribution. Companies with internal IT development teams should also create all their applications with LSB conformance in mind. With this degree of traction, the LSB now has, it is a good idea to ensure that any Linux distribution you select is compliant to the latest version of the LSB and that any applications you acquire are also LSB-compliant. This way, you can be assured that your investment will be preserved.

In many ways, the LSB can be thought of as aggregating a set of standards that the industry uses and the Linux development community endorses. It is actually a stated goal of the LSB to document existing standards and not invent new ones. Since the LSB is not a reinvention of the wheel, but rather built on what is already out there, it has made it very easy for distribution vendors and application providers to work with and comply with the LSB specification.

Since the LSB is a binary specification, it needs to be divided into two core components: general and processor-specific; general for those things that are machine independent, and processor-specific for only those things that must be machine-dependent. Figure 7–1 shows how the two combined on your platform create an LSB-compliant environment for a given architecture.

It is not the goal here to reiterate the entire LSB standard. You can get a copy of the actual specification from the LSB Web site (*www.linuxbase.org/spec*). It is useful to take a high-level view of the standard and how the various components come together.

LSB Distribution Components

The LSB defines the common set of binary interfaces that a conforming application must have available. Figure 7–2 demonstrates the standardized components of an LSB-compliant Linux distribution.

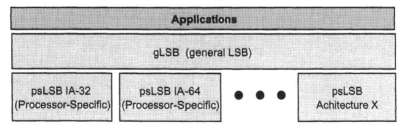

Figure 7–1   LSB architecture support.

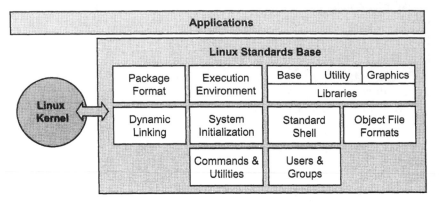

Figure 7–2   LSB-compliant distribution.

Table 7–1 examines each of the significant general LSB (gLSB) elements of a compliant Linux distribution and the impact on applications and deployment:

Table 7–1   Components of gLSB

LSB Component	Description
Linux Kernel Interface	The kernel development teams must be free to innovate and extend the capabilities of the kernel. The LSB was constructed specifically to allow this innovation (more scalability, multithreaded execution models, new scheduling methods, etc.). By specifying a POSIX (a well-established UNIX interface standard) interface, the LSB ensures application compatibility while encouraging innovation. One significant implication of this may be allowing current UNIX implementation to become LSB-compliant.
Package Format	Packaging is the process of combining the collection of files that make up an application together for easy deployment. By defining the packaging format, vendors can select any number of tools that may be created to support the format. End-users can select any tool for deployment of the packages throughout the enterprise.
Dynamic Linking	Dynamic linking specifies the binary format and fields required by applications. Dynamic linking allows many applications to share and reuse functional libraries. By

(continued)

Table 7–1 *(continued)*

LSB Component	Description
Dynamic Linking *(continued)*	specifying the linking format, this ensures that all applications can sharein the reuse model.
Execution Environment	The execution environment is focused on the FSH standard and execution security. As I mentioned, the FSH standard is a key ingredient of the LSB. Ensuring consistency around where files are located within the system allows predictability for applications and system administrators alike.
System Initialization	System initialization recognizes that many applications need to depend on a known state at system startup. This part of the standard ensures that applications have an environment they can count on such as scripts and other configurations.
Standard Shell	Over the years, a number of user shells (the interpreter that executes typed commands at a prompt) have been developed. This part of the standard recognizes the POSIX standard while also recognizing the realities of the most widely used shell in the Linux environment.
Object File Formats	When a compiler creates an executable application from source code, it writes that executable file in a very specific format. By having a clear standard, this ensures that all applications can get loaded and executed by the system.
Libraries	From the chart, you see that there are three core library types: base, graphics, and utilities. Virtually all applications that are loaded on a system are dependent on one or more of the libraries in these categories. Standardizing which libraries must be there ensures that applications can run reliably.
Commands and Utilities	All UNIX and Linux systems ship with hundreds of commands at the disposal of administrators and users. This part of the standard stipulates all the commands and utilities that must be there. This allows applications that are also dependent on scripts to run reliably.
Users and Groups	Again, leveraging the POSIX standard, users, and groups ensures that standards are followed for usernames, certain user IDs, and available groups.

If you recall, the LSB also specifies architecture-specific components. As I mentioned in Chapter 2, since most development occurs on the Intel IA-32 architecture, all of the initial development work starts there. The LSB is no different. At the time of this writing, the LSB architecture-specific module was defined for IA-32 and the draft was in place for IA-64. Table 7–2 lists the components of LSB IA-32:

Table 7–2   Architecture-Specific LSB Components

LSB Component	Description
Low-Level System Information	This section describes the very low-level interface to the IA-32 architecture. This section ensures that compilers have the standards required to create properly executable programs.
Object Format	Similar in context to the gLSB specification, the object format is also directed at the compilers to ensure that symbol information is properly written during compilation.
Program Loading and Dynamic Linking	The act of running a program consists of loading it into memory and scheduling it for execution. As gLSB specifies, during the load phase, applications need to link in any required libraries. This section of the standard ensures that the acts of loading, linking, scheduling, and locating an executable program in memory follow a proper convention.
Base Libraries	Much as gLSB defines a base set of libraries, there are certain libraries that are specific to the IA-32 architecture. These are defined here.

The LSB is a comprehensive standard and set of tools that describes what an application can expect of a compliant system. There are also rules that applications must follow to be considered LSB-compliant.

Conforming Applications

Ensuring that applications you develop, either for internal use or for commercial sale, can run on any Linux distribution is a big win. It will ensure that your users have a choice of Linux distributions to select from, or allow you to change your choice of Linux distributions if you ever need to, thereby protecting your investment.

The simple way to think about application conformance is that your application must run on any LSB-compliant Linux distribution. It cannot be dependent on any vendor extensions that are beyond the scope of the LSB. Also, if your application is combined with or dependent on another application, that other application must also be LSB-compliant.

Of course, your application must conform to all of the object formats and dynamic linking elements outlined in the LSB specification. A little later, we will look at conformance testing so that you make sure your application is LSB-compliant and you know what it means for a distribution to be conformant.

LSB Futures

LSB focused its initial efforts on depth, getting a small subset of all that is Linux very carefully and thoroughly specified. It did so at the expense of breadth. LSB Futures is a subcommittee of the LSB working group. Its goal is to broaden the scope of the LSB to be much more inclusive. If you are motivated to enhance the LSB specification, you should consider joining this group.

Linux Internationalization

The Free Standards Group's second primary working group is the Linux Internationalization Initiative (*www.li18nux.org*), which is focused on standardizing a core set of APIs to ensure that localized applications can run correctly on any LSB Linux distribution.

Distribution vendors benefit from the li18nux standard (the number 18 signifies the number of letters between "i" and "n" in "internationalization") by ensuring that their distribution can be used anywhere in the world, and can run applications from any local region.

Large corporations and ISVs also benefit by being able to localize their applications for any geography while ensuring that their application will run on any compliant distribution.

There are a few terms that are useful to understand:

- **Internationalization**—The process of making an application or other software environment localizable. Internationalization provides the underlying infrastructure to ensure that an application can be localized.

- **Localization**—The process of supporting cultural-specific issues in an application, such as language, time, currency, etc. Once an application's infrastructure has been internationalized, it can then be localized for any number of specific geographies.
- **Globalization**—The combination of internationalization and localization.

When developing applications for internal or commercial use, you should require that all applications be internationalized. By doing this, you will ensure that all of your applications can be localized to your countries of choice when the need arises. It is very common to use third-party companies that specialize in translation services to localize applications for a specific language.

The li18nux standard guides you by providing a standard set of APIs to handle character sets from Latin, Asian, and many other languages. Li18nux also provides test suites and sample implementations for verifying compliance. With li18nux, you will be able to add local support without having to change any code in your applications.

Testing and Conformance

The Free Standards Group takes every opportunity to document and use what already exists. The testing and conformance aspects are really no different. In the UNIX world, the Open Group drives a comprehensive set of test suites to ensure conformance to standards such as UNIX98. The Free Standards Group is working with the Open Group and other skilled UNIX testing organizations to reuse and build on the same test suites rather than starting over. The test suites focused on LSB conformance are divided into four major categories:

- **Distribution testing**—This part of the testing program is directed at Linux distribution vendors. However, there are cases where you may build your own custom distribution for your own internal uses. If you do that, you should make sure that your custom distribution is also LSB-compliant. This ensures that you can run any LSB-compliant application.
- **Application testing**—For ISVs and enterprise customers, this is the most important part of certification testing. Even if your applications are for internal use, you should always check for LSB conformance. This will ensure that you can run your applications on any LSB-compliant distribution that your company chooses to deploy.

- **Build environment testing**—This is also directed at software developers. It makes sure that the environment used for building applications has everything it needs to build LSB-compliant applications.
- **Sample implementation testing**—This is the final method for testing LSB application compliance. By offering a runtime environment that features a minimal "pure" LSB system, application developers can test their applications in a clean, practical method.

Li18nux also has a set of conformance test suites that can be found on their Web site. The Li18nux test suites come in interactive modes, to test visible components of the application, and in automatic mode, to test the proper implementation of the internationalization interfaces.

At the time of this writing, the Free Standards Group was in the process of launching a certification program so that distribution vendors and application vendors could seek a certification seal and use it as part of their marketing campaigns. You should monitor the Free Standards Group Web site on a regular basis to see how this program is evolving and determine when is the right time for you to join.

Specialized Linux Distributions

The standards currently developed and promoted by the Free Standards Group are focused on mainstream Linux distributions. We need to not lose sight of the fact that one of the great strengths of Linux is its ability to be customized at will. There is therefore an endless array of specialized applications (set-top boxes, PDAs, embedded applications, etc.) that will customize Linux to the point where it can no longer be considered "standard." The good news is that as these applications become more and more common, standards efforts will develop to support these environments.

Summary

You have been shown the relevant standards that apply to the mainstream world of Linux. By ensuring that you acquire and deploy LSB-compliant distributions and follow through with LSB-compliant applications, you should take advantage of the key Linux benefit that avoids vendor lock-in. For large corporations and software vendors, following the li18nux specification for globalization ensures that you can deliver your applications in whatever local markets justify the expense of localization.

Operations—Using Linux and Open Source

*F*or Linux to become real in your environment, it needs to become an integral part of your day-to-day operations. For most businesses, this means having a plan to deploy Linux in an existing infrastructure. Those of you who choose to migrate from an existing UNIX or Windows environment to Linux need to understand what a migration and coexistence plan should include. The latter part of this chapter will cover some of the other operational elements that will likely be different for Linux: support and training.

This chapter covers operational elements. Since every enterprise is different, you should think of this chapter as a tool to help you make decisions and choices for deploying Linux in your environment. This chapter does not attempt to present a case for migrating from UNIX, Windows, or any other operating environment to Linux, but rather presents the elements you should consider to help you make that choice, or if you have already made that choice, the elements to help you plan for a successful implementation. There are cases when migrating to Linux is not appropriate and should not be considered.

Deployment

Deploying Linux in your enterprise will require extensive planning to decide which applications to implement on Linux first. In most cases, Linux will need to be deployed alongside an existing infrastructure. Even if you were to decide to become a pure Linux shop, it would likely take months, or even years, to accomplish that goal.

To deploy Linux in your enterprise, first decide which Linux distribution you will deploy and how you will package it. If you recall the details of the distribution chapter, you will likely find yourself creating a custom distribution. You will then need to package your image so that you have a consistent deployment that you can support in your environment. Next, look at the variety of open source and commercial deployment and management tools available to help you make your solution successful. You will obviously need to test the specific application to make sure it meets all of your performance, reliability, and scalability requirements.

Most distribution vendors also offer services (usually involving monthly fees) that will automatically update your deployments when new features or bug fixes are available. For small businesses, or the individual user, these automatic update services can be a great service that offers tremendous convenience. However, for most medium and large enterprises, these update services need to be brought in-house and integrated with the IT environment. This will allow you to test updates and fixes with your specific applications to ensure that no other side-effects are encountered and that you can stage an update properly for mass deployment throughout the organization. Work with your distribution vendor to develop the specifics that will work in your environment.

Every enterprise deployment will be unique, and it is not possible for me to consider each individual case. However, there are a number of issues associated with migration, coexistence, and other operational elements that each enterprise should consider.

Geographic Deployments

If your company has offices in a number of different countries, you will need to make a choice of which distributions to deploy on this worldwide scale. You learned in Chapter 5 that many distributions have a geographic focus, or heritage. It is highly likely that your employees in these offices will be familiar with this local distribution, and even have a strong desire to favor them for deployment. The other likely scenario is that these distributions of local interest will be the only ones that have been localized in the native culture and language.

You can make a choice to standardize on a single distribution for all your deployments around the world, or you can make the decision to let your remote offices make a local choice. This is where one of the beauties of the LSB standard comes into play. By focusing your energy on

LSB compliance, you can leverage the geographic presence of local distribution providers and ensure that all of your corporate application choices will work throughout the organization.

Migration and Coexistence

As I mentioned at the start of this chapter, my intent is not to make the case for migrating. There are a number of resources available on the Internet (some of them listed in the reference section) dedicated to the specific issues of migrating from one platform to another given very specific circumstances. It would be easy to dedicate an entire book to the details of migration issues from the platform, through to the application, and the overall environment. My intent here is to cover the significant migration issues you should consider at the platform and operating system layers.

Migration will involve costs. For a migration to be viable, you must be able to justify the costs with substantial new gains. For this reason, if you have a stable environment that is meeting your business needs at minimal costs, a migration may not make any sense. Some of the more significant migration costs to consider are:

- **Hardware**—Moving to Linux may involve a change of hardware platforms. Depending on the current age of your existing systems, this may or may not make sense. On the other hand, as you will discover a little later, Linux's ability to support multiple platforms can make hardware reuse an attractive proposition.
- **Training**—If your current environment is predominantly based on UNIX systems, then the retraining of your administrative staff should be minimal. If, however, you are migrating from a Windows, Novell, or other environment, the retraining costs will be considerable.
- **Licensing**—Depending on the applications you use and your current environment, you may need to repurchase or upgrade many of your current applications. This assumes that your business applications are available for Linux. On the plus side, since Linux itself has no licensing fees, you may be able to offset some of these costs.
- **Data**—It is highly likely that your true assets are in the information you store rather than the hardware and software used to store and retrieve that information. When transitioning an existing environment, data migration can become the highest cost and highest risk element. I will cover some elements of data migration a little later.

To fully understand the impacts of migration, we need to look at the details of the key components that affect these costs.

Hardware

There are those who believe that since Linux can run on a wide range of different architectures, you should consider active deployment on any of those architectures. In Chapter 2, I outlined a number of reasons why deploying Linux on hardware platforms other than the ones where the core development occurs can be undesirable. However, migration and hardware reuse can present a good opportunity for Linux on non-core development platforms. Assume that you have an existing hardware platform that is based on a proprietary architecture. Your end goal is to deploy Linux on industry-standard hardware. Such a move will likely not occur overnight. Therefore, you can take some effective steps to reuse your existing hardware to make that transition over a number of months, or even years.

Figure 8–1 presents a simplistic view of the steps needed to get from a pure proprietary environment to a pure open, standard environment. Obviously, the real work involved in each of these steps can be very complex. If the proprietary operating system is UNIX-based, then the transition of the applications, scripts, and other components of your software infrastructure can be minimal. Other non-UNIX operating systems such as VMS, MVS, and others could require significant rewrites before being able to run on Linux. The one difficulty with Step 1 will be commercial applications. Since most commercial software vendors will make their applications available only on industry-standard hardware architectures, getting a version for your current proprietary hardware could be difficult. For these situations, you should use the approach demonstrated here as a first step in the migration of all your internally developed applications and scripts and leave commercial applications for the final stage of migration to industry-standard hardware.

In the second step, changing the hardware will likely involve environmental considerations. Does your environment have the right type of power, cooling, space, etc. to support different hardware than you have used in the past? You will also need to consider connectivity issues. In some cases, you might be able to reuse the I/O interfaces of your proprietary hardware in your open architecture systems. In other cases, you may have to repurchase this hardware. You must consider all the network and storage connectivity on which your current infrastructure is based (there

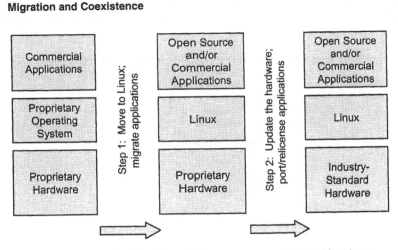

Figure 8–1 Migrating to Linux on open, standard hardware.

may be other peripheral connections as well). When changing the hardware platform, the performance, scalability, and reliability characteristics will all change (some for the better, and some for the worse). You should take the time to understand the end-user and business impacts that these changes will have.

Data

Data migration will be an important consideration, especially if your current data is shared among many systems in your current environment. Data migration will involve storage formats, sharing between systems, and application data. One of the first considerations is the Endian byte order being used by your current system.

Endian

In Jonathan Swift's book, *Gulliver's Travels*, Swift describes the inhabitants of Lilliput who break their eggs on the larger side as Big-Endians. We can assume that those who break their eggs on the smaller side would be Little-Endians. The term "Endian" has been borrowed by the computer industry to refer to a difference in byte order used by various computers and operating systems. Endian byte order, shown in Figure 8–2, refers to the direction in which bytes of data are stored and retrieved by a system. If a system has stored data using big-Endian byte order, and the new system retrieves it in little-Endian byte order, then data corruption is assured. Your goal is to prevent this with proper planning.

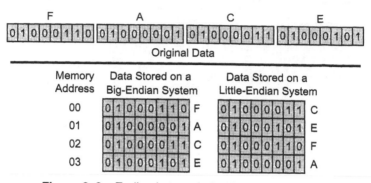

Figure 8–2   Endian byte ordering for 32-bit systems.

Any operating system/microprocessor combination can have a different Endian byte order. Linux on the IA-32 and IA-64 platforms is little-Endian, while Linux on SPARC and PA-RISC is big-Endian. HP-UX on PA-RISC and Solaris on SPARC are big-Endian, while Solaris on IA-32 is little-Endian. This byte order issue is often the most overlooked, least understood in any migration effort.

As you can see from the example, Linux is ambidextrous when it comes to Endian byte order. It depends on the architectural implementation. For this reason, most Linux developers will consider an application that is Endian-sensitive (or Endian-unaware) as broken, or defective. The Linux development community has developed a set of small, easy-to-use tools to ensure that applications developed for Linux are not Endian-sensitive. This is part of the reason why Linux applications port easily between architectures.

Most commercial applications that have already been ported to other platforms will likely have already dealt with this issue. This means that any internal application data will not be sensitive to Endian issues and you will be able to use the same data even if you move your application from a proprietary system to Linux or between Linux systems. You should pay special consideration to internally developed applications. Very often, internal IT applications will not have considered Endian issues and porting your internal applications will need to be extensively tested for data corruption.

File Systems

In earlier chapters, I went through some of the various file systems available for Linux. The most common in use today is the ext2 file system (and most recently, ext3 extensions for journaling). If you are migrating from UNIX systems, you need to understand what file system you are currently using, and if that file system is available for Linux. File systems are often integral to high-availability structures to make sure that if a system failure occurs, backup systems will continue to have data available. If you are migrating or coexisting with Windows-based systems, you will likely need to move your data to the new storage file system you have chosen for Linux. Fortunately, the open source community has developed drivers for all of the Microsoft file systems. This will ensure that you can access your data that may reside on a Windows system on your Linux system.

There are far too many open, proprietary, and commercial file systems available to list here, with new ones continuously being developed. The odds are very good that the open source community has already developed drivers for many of the proprietary file systems. Many of the commercial vendors delivering sophisticated file systems for proprietary operating systems have also made versions of their file systems available for Linux.

Sharing

Closely related to file systems are file and print sharing systems. These sharing systems allow users on a network to share files, printers, and other resources on a network. This allows an enterprise to make effective use of expensive infrastructure components. The most common way that corporations share printers and files is through the use of Microsoft protocols. These protocols are Common Internet File System (CIFS) and Server Message Block (SMB). UNIX platforms have traditionally shared files through the networked file system, or NFS. The good news is that the open source community (and some commercial vendors) has developed solutions for interoperability between these very important protocols. Figure 8–3 represents how these file and print sharing services interact on a network.

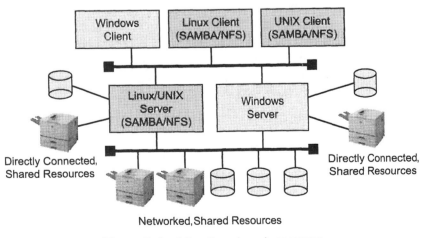

Figure 8–3   Migrating shared resources.

SAMBA (an expansion of the SMB acronym) is one of the great open source technologies that will allow your Linux (and UNIX) systems to co-exist with your Windows environment and share resources. You can make the choice to migrate servers and clients at the pace that makes the most sense for your business. SAMBA has both a client implementation and a server implementation. If you implement a SAMBA server on your existing Windows network, it will appear as just another server to all of your Windows clients.

If your infrastructure is highly dependent on the NFS protocol, it is also possible to run this protocol on Linux and Windows systems. Most NFS implementations for Windows are available from commercial third-party vendors.

The combination of SAMBA and NFS allows you create an unlimited number of integration points between Windows, Linux, and UNIX systems as well as any other system that understands these core protocols. This allows you to plan an orderly migration to the ideal, most cost-effective platform for your environment.

Programming Models

Programming models refer to the APIs that application developers use to create applications that run on the chosen operating system. Since UNIX and Linux share a very close heritage and very similar programming models, application developers can usually adapt to the Linux programming model very easily. In fact, Linux is sometimes considered the lowest common denominator for all UNIX-based systems.

The programming model for Windows systems is based on a core API known as Win32. This model is dramatically different than the model used by Linux and UNIX systems. Since the programming paradigm is so fundamentally different, developers from one environment usually struggle quite a bit to move to the other. If you have an extensive talent base familiar with the Win32 programming model, you should expect a steep and difficult learning curve for most of your developers attempting to absorb the Linux program model. This difficult change will be similar for most other non-UNIX operating systems.

If most of the development within your organization is based on higher level development paradigms such as Java application servers or database applications, then the switch to a different programming model at the operating system layer could be painless and even invisible for your developers.

Applications

When migrating from existing proprietary environments to a Linux-based platform, you should look for open source equivalents to your existing applications. This is not meant to promote the notion that all open source software can replace any commercial application. Rather, there are times when we implement very good and very powerful commercial applications, but end up using a very small percentage of the capabilities of the software. If you have deployed applications that are not being used to the full extent of their capabilities, there may be an open source equivalent out there that more than meets your requirements. For example, you may be using a commercial database to do simple storage and retrieval of employee data on an internal Web portal. The odds are quite good that an open source database such as MySQL or PostGRES will more than meet your needs.

Desktop

Migrating a desktop environment to Linux should be undertaken with some degree of care. Most will agree that the Linux desktop is currently suited primarily to power users, or engineers accustomed to UNIX desktops. While this may change as time progresses, evolving your desktop environment for an average user will require some extensive retraining, not only on the operating system itself (user interface, file sharing, file management, etc.), but also on all of the office productivity applications currently in use within your infrastructure. If you make the choice to migrate your office productivity desktop environment to Linux, make sure that you have a detailed inventory of all the applications that your users currently depend on, and also make sure that even your Web-based applications will work with Linux-based Web browsers.

There are also a number of solutions appearing on the market based on an open project called "WINE" (Win32 Emulator). Win32 is the core Windows operating system API. WINE has been developed to provide this API on the Linux operating system. WINE allows a few select Windows based applications to run as-is on your system. Commercial vendors are certifying and testing specific applications and providing special installation tools to help the process of loading and running applications.

Licensing and Purchasing

Licenses for commercial software running on a Linux system are largely unchanged from those of any other platform. Some software vendors have tried to correlate the cost of the hardware platform and operating system to the cost of the application running on that platform. In most cases, there is very little reason to expect that correlation. In fact, the price/performance cost of hardware has reduced dramatically over the years, but the cost of commercial software has largely stayed the same or even increased over the same period. The price of commercial software should be based on the competitive landscape and the value it delivers to its customers, not on the price of the hardware on which it runs.

If you are migrating from an existing proprietary platform to a Linux system, you should contact your commercial software suppliers to ensure that the applications you need to run your business are available on Linux and that they are all LSB-compliant. You will then need to negotiate the price of moving those licenses from your current platform to your new Linux system. As I mentioned in the previous section, there may be instances where the availability of an open source competitive offering will create more favorable price points, or you may be able to consider an open source alternative to an existing application.

If you implement open source applications, then you should ensure that your procurement group is well aware that freely copying open source software for use throughout your enterprise is perfectly legal. Your purchasing agents need to clearly understand the difference between procuring open source software as opposed to any bundled add-ons that a vendor may be including with the open source software. This does not mean that there is no value in the bundles, or the add-ons. However, since the process for purchasing commercial, proprietary software is well-understood, there may be a tendency to apply the same process to open source software. Make sure when you work with your open source software vendors that you are clear about the price for the specific components (media, support, manuals, etc.) for which you are paying. In some cases, hardware vendors will include Linux bundles or other open source software and may be charging to cover their costs in including this software. You should uncover these costs in detail and decide if the convenience associated with these bundles is worth the cost. Take the time to train your purchasing agents on the details of how open source works so that they can get the best possible advantage for your company.

Support

The support model for Linux and open source software can change dramatically from your current model, or it can stay relatively static. The good news here is that the choice is largely yours. The available support models can be thought of in these general categories:

- Commercial by component
- Integrated end-to-end
- Self-support with the community

Since these support models are likely to be very different from your current models, it is worth going through each one in detail.

Commercial by Component

This model uses a different commercial vendor for each component of your solution stack. The hardware support is delivered by the hardware vendor, the operating system support by the distribution vendor, the application support by the commercial supplier of the open source application, and so on.

The main advantage to this support model is that if any vendor support in the stack does not measure up to your expectations, you can change that component, or the support for that component, without necessarily affecting other parts of the stack. The other logic to this model is that it delivers best-of-breed support for each component of the solution.

This model can also make a lot of sense for branded or commercialized open source solutions such as a Linux distribution. For example, if you deploy a Linux distribution from one of the major vendors, that vendor will usually be in the best position to make changes to the distribution should you encounter any difficulties. In some cases, you can even take advantage of competitive support offerings for any individual component. The same model applies for other branded or commercialized open source software products.

While this model is preferred by many enterprises implementing Linux and open source solutions, it can present some disadvantages:

- **Solution ownership**—Building a support model based on each individual component can deliver best-of-breed. However, there are cases when you will encounter difficulties and the source of the problem is not obvious. You may then find yourself managing conflicts between component suppliers.

- **Component upgrades**—Managing each vendor and each support contract means that you take ownership for the overall solution working together. If you upgrade any one component, you can create a situation where another vendor in the stack will refuse to support a component. In this model, you should ensure that you have a clear articulation from each vendor in the solution as to what they will support and how they plan to manage conflict resolution.
- **Contract management**—This model necessitates that you manage a number of different support contracts, each with their own independent terms. If you do not have the management infrastructure to manage each contract, this may not be the best model for your business.

You need to make sure you consider the disadvantages as much as the advantages so that you have a complete reflection of the benefits of your deployment.

Integrated End-to-End

This is the polarized opposite of commercial by component. In this model, you apply the support model of one vendor delivering end-to-end support for your solution. The advantages here should be obvious. You hold one single vendor responsible for the overall functioning of the deployment. Within this model, there is a mix of processes that your selected vendor can use to support your business. In one model, since your vendor is supporting open source software, that vendor can take the role of making whatever changes are required to the software to fix any problems you might encounter. Alternatively, your vendor can take the role of prime contractor and sub-contract the support of individual components to commercial vendors of open source software.

Regardless of the model, your selected support vendor needs to be able to demonstrate influence points within the open source community. This influence is critical since the vendor needs to have the ability to fix problems in such a way that changes are incorporated into the primary source repository under the control of the maintainer.

Self-Support with the Community

Larger IT organizations may choose to support themselves, or combine self-support with some degree of commercial support as an effective way to control costs. This model requires a highly trained and competent technical team. The key will also be to ensure that your internal support team has the freedom to build relationships with key players of the open source community. Your objective should be to meet your support goals, while helping the community you work with be successful and make forward progress. Getting close to the community and developing influence points should not be used as an underhanded attempt at gaining favors; it will backfire. It needs to be regarded as a true symbiotic relationship, where both partners develop a positive interdependency that benefits both parties. In short, you should be working toward a "win-win" situation between your company and the open source community.

If you combine self-support with commercial support, then the model will usually take the form of individuals in your organization taking a lead role in identifying the specific source of whatever problem is encountered. Identification should often lead to actual code fixes submitted to the project maintainer. Then, working with your commercial vendor of open source software, encourage them to include the fixes that have been submitted to the maintainer within their commercial release. Until a new commercial release is viable, you will also need to develop an agreement that your commercial vendor will support the fix as a patch to the commercial implementation.

One of the key benefits of this support model is that you take an active role and direct control over any issues that you may encounter. In a typical proprietary support model, you are completely at the mercy of the vendor's perception of how critical any given issue might be. This model allows you to make the decision for yourself, make the investment to actually implement a change or fix, and then work directly with the developer to implement that change. As long as your fix or change is consistent with the architectural direction of the project, any maintainer will be more than happy to accept your changes (assuming you have developed a reputation for quality contributions).

Influence and Relationships

Regardless of which support model you choose to implement, success all boils down to influence and relationships. The question becomes one of knowing who will develop relationships with the key maintainers within the community. You can choose to leave this responsibility to other vendors, take complete control, or take any combination of these two models.

This is part of the fundamental value proposition of open source software: the ability to take control of your environment and take advantage of a competitive support infrastructure. There will be some companies that have become so accustomed to a dependence on a proprietary support model that it will be very difficult for them to adapt to a type of support structure that is dependent on personal relationships and a web of influence. If you wish to take advantage of the benefits of open source, but have difficulty with an influence-based support model, then you should work with commercial vendors that have a proven track record of close ties with relevant communities.

Training

Most operating system vendors have developed certification programs to allow companies to recognize a level of competence in the environment. Standardized training is a big win for everyone involved. For the operating system vendor, it ensures that IT professionals are focused and competent in making any installation as successful as possible. For IT shops, it provides an effective way to recruit and identify talent that can deploy and support the infrastructure. For individuals, it clearly outlines a curriculum that will ensure they are learning the topics that will add value to an organization.

Like almost everything else in the open source community, the need for standardized, vendor-neutral Linux training spawned a new subcommunity: the Linux Professional Institute, or LPI (*www.lpi.org*). The LPI defines three levels of certification: The first level defines a level suitable for power users and help desk support; the second level of certification is for those planning and implementing small IT networks; and the third level is intended for senior IT architects who define, design, and implement large, multisite enterprises.

There are other recognized training programs for Linux such as CompTIA (*www.comptia.org*) and SAIR Linux GNU certification (*www.linuxcertification.org*). Also, some Linux distribution vendors have developed certification programs specific to their distributions. Your company should examine the details of each certification program and decide which one(s) to officially recognize. This will help you to decide what program to follow for existing employees, and what programs to look for during the recruiting process for new talent.

While most of these certification programs will include training for components included with most Linux distributions such as SAMBA and the Apache Web Server, these certification programs will not include training for every conceivable open source project. Once you have identified which open source projects will be implemented and deployed within your organization, you should look for training programs that may be available for each project. Alternatively, you can easily develop training programs internally. This is another benefit of open source technologies. Since the source code is available for any project, you can develop training programs to virtually any degree of depth your company desires. You could even resell the training and make money from open source.

Finally, there is open source training. This is training on licenses and processes that employees should follow when using or implementing open source software in your organization. Part 3 of this book will outline detailed processes for using open source software within your organization, as well as potentially releasing your software under an open source license. Training your employees on the details of these processes is an important component of your overall training curriculum.

Summary

This chapter completes your foundation of Linux knowledge and some open source elements. You should now have a deeper understanding of the core operational elements involved with a successful Linux deployment. Obviously, migrating from an existing UNIX environment tends to be the simplest of evolutions, but more and more companies are also being successful migrating from operating environments of a completely different heritage.

Now that you have a solid foundation in Linux, it is time to discover that Linux is simply a significant instance of an open source project. So far, I have hinted numerous times at the fact that much of what you were learning applied not only to Linux, but all open source projects. Part 3 explores open source in great detail and gives you all you need to extend your specific Linux capabilities into any open source project.

Open Source
in Business

*P*art 3 takes a detailed look at all of the different business elements that need to be reconsidered as a result of the open source paradigm. "Open source" is a broad term that covers licensing, development processes, culture, and many other elements. Integrating an open source mindset within your company will be a complex and difficult task, but it will be an accomplishment that will bring many rewards if you do it right.

The first chapter in Part 3 starts by examining the open source development process as though it lived within corporate walls. This association should help the uninitiated get a sense for the culture and style of development. The next chapter looks at the economic effect of open source software on traditional business models. The natural extension in the following chapter is to take a detailed look at open source business models. Chapter 12 will detail the business processes of moving some of your software to an open source license as well as integrating open source software in your business. The final component of open source will be to examine the human resources aspect, detailing the impact on employment and how to hire the best talent.

CHAPTER 9

The Corporate Bazaar

I often say, "It's not about Linux; it's about open source," or more precisely, the open source development process. This is the style of development that Eric Raymond has labeled the "bazaar" development style, and it is the real magic behind Linux. In this chapter, we will extend the bazaar development style to the corporation. Your goals for this chapter are to understand:

- The differences between "cathedral" and "bazaar" development styles
- The theoretical structure of a bazaar in the corporation
- How to gain the advantages of a bazaar development style

One of the key things to keep in mind as you read this chapter is that this discussion does not have anything to do with making your development project public. Separate in your mind the notion of open source as a group of licenses that you can use to release your software and open source as a software development style. This chapter is about the development style and has nothing to do with releasing your source under any open source license. Chapter 12 will walk you through the detailed process of "going public" with your development project, or using public code within your internal projects.

Explaining the open source development methodology to a seasoned corporate manager can be quite difficult. Therefore, the process I use in this chapter is to theorize what a corporate structure might look like if it was imposed on the community. This has two advantages: 1) It presents the development methodology in terms that should be somewhat more familiar; and 2) it should challenge you to rethink all or parts of how you do software development in your organization.

The Cathedral and the Bazaar

This terminology comes from the groundbreaking paper by Eric Raymond. In it, he defines traditional software development, which you most likely understand very well, as the cathedral style of development. He describes the new open source development process pioneered by Linus Torvalds as a bazaar development style. It is not my intention to review the entire contents of Eric's paper here, but it is important that you have a high-level understanding of what the cathedral and the bazaar represent.

- **Cathedral development**—This is the traditional style of development where teams are kept small. The design and functionality are well-understood before development begins. Complete plans from architecture, design, development, integration, and test are well-understood and documented. Release cycles during the development phase are few, and external feedback is only sought during alpha and beta test cycles.
- **Bazaar development**—A maintainer releases functionality that can be built and has some usefulness, but the package lacks functionality and defects may be prevalent. Release cycles are frequent (sometimes hourly). Feedback is sought as early and as frequently as possible. Anyone, anywhere, with a good idea can contribute to either fix defects or add interesting new functionality. The maintainer declares a production release when he or she determines it is ready.

These are summary descriptions. Obviously, I strongly encourage you to read Eric's paper (and book). Eric's thesis attempted to replicate what Linus accomplished with Linux. Eric was able to replicate it on a different project, but his parameters were very similar to those of Linus': He was working with a public community of volunteers. What Eric did not address was how to take all the benefits of bazaar development and bring them to the corporate world. The question here is how one takes into account the structural realities of large corporations today. Real issues come into focus: management hierarchies, personal career goals, human resources regulations, equipment availability, and a strategic context defined by executive management, not to mention competitive pressures faced by the company.

Structure Follows Strategy

Before we go into a functional model, it is important to understand goals and strategies. Many unseasoned managers have made the mistake of building organizational and functional structures before knowing or understanding company strategy. It is not possible for me to understand the individual company strategies for every reader, but there are some common goals and objectives, as well as development strategies, that can be applied generically. If you attempt to apply the bazaar development style in your company, it will be useful to review the benefits of bazaar development in the open source community:

- **Rapid development**—Most will agree that the open source community has achieved very impressive development cycles. Linux has evolved to be a modern, credible operating system in less than 10 years. Not one, but two comprehensive GUIs, GNOME and KDE, have been developed in less than five years. And of course, we cannot neglect the success of *the* open source killer application: the Apache Web Server.
- **Distributed development**—The only reason Linux and Apache could be developed as rapidly as they were is because of the Internet infrastructure that developed in parallel. The community leveraged this communications infrastructure to the point where many developments took place with developers on a project never meeting face to face. This ability to develop in a distributed fashion leveraged time zone benefits and granted access to talent no matter where it might reside.
- **Best of talent**—The community is well-known for having a low tolerance for poor contributions. If you don't make substantive contributions (code, design, architecture, test, documentation, etc.) somewhere, the community does not want you. While I have not been able to find anyone in the community who looks at this in this way, I interpret this as *built-in talent management*. Talent management is often one of the most difficult aspects of management inside corporations today.

- **Meeting user needs**—One of the most interesting dynamics in the open source community is that *the developer is the user*. It is therefore not too difficult to extrapolate from that assertion to understand why the end product tends to meet the user's needs. Within your company, this fact requires an acceptance that your developers are users, and their input to the project is significant.
- **Quality**—The expression "Given enough eyeballs, all bugs are shallow" started with Eric's paper and now has been echoed throughout the community. The seemingly out-of-control style of open source development yields some of the best quality software around. In this case, quality applies to a system that is running within the parameters it was architected and designed for. Experienced software development managers will assert that quality begins with a well-understood architecture. If the needs of the user extend beyond the architecture of the system, then you will often need to rewrite many components of the application. For quality to extend from architecture to running code, a visionary is required to guide the system.

This is an impressive list of benefits. I cannot think of too many executives who would not like to benefit from every item on this list. However, the detractors of this development style usually point to some flaws that prevent the system from being successful within a company:

- **Market requirements**—It is fine to say that the developer is the user, but many consumers are not developers. As a result, the end product will not meet the actual needs of the customer.
- **Roadmap**—I think we have all been conditioned to think of our development projects on a roadmap that provides a communication vehicle for many within and outside the company. It also sets expectations that others can use to work on their projects. The idea that developers release when ready is difficult for management, or the Marketing Department, to swallow.
- **People management**—Who manages these developers who are making all these wonderful contributions? What process provides the guidance? Managing a team of developers who might be contributing to projects that are not part of their organizational structure is a difficult cultural effect to internalize.

All these drawbacks tend to boil down to management's desire to be in control and be able to make commitments they can stand behind. What you are about to learn is how you can give up that fundamental control and end up delivering more product with more functionality, and a higher degree of quality than you ever had before. As an added bonus, you will get a workforce that is highly optimized to your business and loves what they do.

Structural Bazaar

Now that you have an understanding of the goals you would like to achieve, and you also understand the potential issues, I can give you a functional model, which is depicted in Figure 9-1. This is a generic model that assumes a fairly large software development team (more than 100 engineers). It does not matter if you are developing a small product for commercial use or a large IT project for internal use. *Remember that for this chapter, your goal is not to release your code to the public. You are trying to bring all the benefits of collaborative development in-house.*

This gives you a big picture of the elements in a collaborative software development structure. From this functional structure, you will need to develop the organizational structure that best mirrors these functions. Before we go into the details of each part of this structure, take a quick note of some of the key elements that might be different from your company. For example, notice that all the engineering talent lives in one place rather than being a distinct part of the hierarchy. Also notice that much of the personnel development takes place within human resources rather than within a management chain. All this will soon make sense.

As we go through each part of this structure, imagine that your job is to deliver a functioning Linux operating system (your real job might be to deliver a portal, a database, or any number of products). The point is for you to be able to connect how the community does development to how you can accomplish the same thing. By pretending that you are actually developing the Linux operating system, you can imagine the one-for-one linkage between the open source community and your organization. As you will see, there are places where there are no linkages. *That is the point.* You have to recognize that there will be differences, but do not let those differences keep you away from reaping the benefits. You will also gain key insights into how the community does development.

This structure does not deal with certain other structural issues such as sales, manufacturing, and support. We will cover some of the impacts on these functions near the end of this chapter.

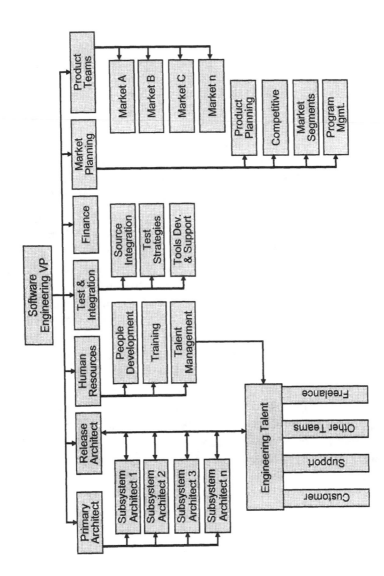

Figure 9–1 Functional model for corporate open source development.

Software Engineering VP

Do not get too hung up on the title. The intent here is to reference the top-level executive responsible for the overall delivery of the product to market. The VP's job is to provide the strategic context for what is being developed and be the person leading the desired initiative. For example, are we developing a Linux kernel, an Apache Web Server, or a MySQL database? There is usually a need to connect this development activity to other projects or initiatives within the company. For example, how do multiple projects inter-relate? With the core staff outlined on the chart, the VP also has all the key elements required to make sure there is alignment within the organization. The key questions become:

- Is the market planning team communicating effectively with engineering teams? Are they going after the right markets?
- Is the human resources group able to acquire the talent required to get the job done?
- Is the product being developed properly focused, on the identified market segments?
- Is the company meeting its revenue targets for each of the specified markets?
- Is the innovation keeping pace (or accelerating faster) with the market?
- Are all the components we need for a whole product there and being delivered?
- Is product quality acceptable? Are we responding to defects at an acceptable rate?
- Is the product meeting the needs of the users within the identified segments?
- Is the organization executing within the cost/revenue envelope specified?
- Is the morale of the organization fostering an energized team?
- Are we keeping the best available talent?

Think of these as the executive dashboard. At the end of the day, you want to be delivering the best, most innovative product possible, with the highest possible quality, and with a healthy profit. These three elements become the catalysts for team dynamics. If the team is winning, the team will deliver ever-increasing levels of greatness.

There is one other key responsibility of the VP. You will shortly learn that the primary architect makes the final call on when the technology is ready for release. In most companies, there will be extreme pressure and influence coming from all directions to release sooner. The VP *must* stand by the primary architect's decision. In the early days of adopting a bazaar development style, this will be extremely difficult. It completely contradicts most corporate management structures and tends to invoke corporate immune systems. As you demonstrate a leading-edge product in the market, the pressure will subside, but never completely disappear.

Technology Team

Based on the structure shown, the technology team is composed of the primary architect, the release architect, and the engineering talent. There is another part of the technology team that I will talk about later, the "go-to-market" team. The technology team is responsible for delivering the core technology, not the polished product. That will fall on the go-to-market team. For now, let's go through the key roles in the technology team, and some of the resultant dynamics.

Primary Architect

The primary architect should be the lead visionary. This might be somewhat different than a typical Chief Technology Officer (CTO) role in large companies. Whereas the CTO would generally be responsible for the overall company technology vision, the primary architect drives the vision for a given product. In our case, we want to deliver the Linux operating system. What are the key strategic goals? Performance? Scalability? Usability? Networkability? If all of these are goals, then what is the priority, and what are the tradeoffs?

Some argue that technologists are incapable of internalizing customer needs and market requirements. The open source community has proven that this assertion is patently false. You must draw on the fact that one of the key motivators for any software engineer is having his or her stuff in production use. Yes, there are some engineers who will be mesmerized by cool technology, but those in this category who do are best left lower within the hierarchy. Those who mature beyond the coolness of the technology will be your future architects.

The goal is to guide your primary architect with a key set of measures and metrics that will ensure the right balance of innovation and product competitiveness. Here are the key metrics you should develop, specific to your company:

- Is the currently released product competitive relative to its peers in the market?
- Does the product meet the established customer satisfaction goals (features, quality, performance, etc.)?
- Is the technology being developed innovative? Are there enough key differentiators to distinguish you from the pack?

It should not be the objective to make the primary architect swim on his or her own. The architect needs help, and this is where the market planning teams should come in. The goal is to give your architect access to as much information as needed to make successful decisions. A mature architect will thrive on this access to the information.

The primary architect must also define the subsystem boundaries. Any large software development project will be divided into subsystems. The goal is to develop an architecture that builds the fewest interdependencies between subsystems as possible. Where the dependencies cannot be eliminated, the architect must clearly define the interfaces to be used for subsystem interaction. By having clearly defined boundaries, the primary architect can delegate the ownership of a subsystem to a trusted lieutenant.

The primary architect is also responsible for accepting all code submissions from subsystem architects. Since the metrics listed earlier hold the primary architect accountable for the final product, the architect will be highly motivated to build a trusted team of subsystem architects. This is where talent management begins, which is based on a hierarchy of trust. If a subsystem does not meet expectations, then a new subsystem architect will rapidly get named. The primary architect should get all the flexibility needed to make that call. If that flexibility is lost, you have returned to a "cathedral" development style. The degree of tolerance for bad submissions at this level should be extremely low. The primary architect must balance the need to deliver a competitive product on a timely basis with the consequences of delivering a product that is of poor quality or does not meet the needs of the stated market.

The primary architect also determines when the technology is ready for release. This determination will be based on any number of factors, including quality, features, performance, and others. In the end, the architect is the one accountable and must make the final choice. If the release is too soon, then the technology won't be competitive. If the release is too late, then competitors will begin to take market share. This counterbalancing set of elements will guide the right release point. You will need to decide what rewards and consequences you can use to motivate the right decision. Make sure that motivations are not deceitful or manipulative, or they will backfire. You must understand that it is not the job of the primary architect to be the only genius behind the complete system. It is the job of all the architects (including the primary architect) in the technology team to recognize the genius of others and shamelessly incorporate it while ensuring that due credit is given.

Finally, the primary architect must maintain an almost symbiotic relationship with the release architect. Once the technology is released, it will be the job of the release architect to make minor repairs and enhancements to the system. There must be an implicit level of trust between these two architects since the release architect will be in a position to make decisions that affect the future design and architecture of the overall system. This is similar to Linus and Marcello working on the Linux kernel.

Release Architect

The release architect should be viewed as the primary architect in waiting. You can also think of this as the disaster recovery plan. Although it is always possible to replace the primary architect with anyone with the right skill set, having the release architect role provides a needed redundancy in the system and avoids a state of limbo if the primary architect is suddenly no longer part of your organization. Many people have asked, "What happens to Linux if Linus Torvalds gets run over by a bus?" This is how the community has built a fail-safe system. Marcello can be immediately available to keep Linux going, even if the community at large chooses a completely different maintainer for the long term.

After the primary architect has released the technology to the rest of the organization for productization, the release architect takes over. No matter the quality of the system, there will always be the occasional defect or critical feature that needs to get done. In some systems, security holes might be discovered that need immediate attention. The release architect is responsible for the reactive response to system issues after the software is released. However, the release architect must maintain the overall architectural purity of the system. If submissions or suggestions are made that involve a fundamental architectural change to the system, then the submission should be forwarded to the primary architect for consideration in a future release.

As you can see from the functional chart, the release architect works with the same subsystem architects as the primary architect. It is important that there be single points of control for each subsystem. Also, the knowledgeable talent for the particular subsystem will be familiar to the subsystem architect. We will discuss the subsystem architect's role in more detail shortly, then we will go through the details of how the release architect can motivate the set of teams to help solve problems on the released technology when it counts.

In many ways, the release architect has a more difficult job than the primary architect. He or she must know as much about the architecture as the primary architect. He or she must keep track of the same market dynamics. In short, he or she needs to nearly clone the primary architect, yet he or she does not have the ability to change the fundamental architecture of the system.

The metrics for your release architect focus on responsiveness and quality. Measuring the speed at which the release architect can deliver critical updates to the system ensures that most of the other elements required for success are there. For example, if the release architect does not maintain his or her knowledge of the overall system, responsiveness will suffer. Similarly, if he or she cannot maintain the requisite relationships with the other team players, he or she will not be able to get the needed changes into the system. Measuring quality ensures that speed is balanced with customer satisfaction.

Subsystem Architects

The subsystem architects are in fact a hierarchy of architects, or senior system developers. The depth of the hierarchy will depend on the complexity of the system. For the purposes of this discussion, assume only one layer. If there are multiple layers, then the uppermost layer performs a similar function to the primary architect by accepting complete contributions from the underlying subsystems.

If you think about the technology behind the Linux operating system, you can rapidly think about a number of subsystems: virtual memory, file systems, process manager, and networking, just to name a few. As I mentioned earlier, the boundaries of these subsystems are defined by the primary architect and may change as the overall system evolves. It should not be a goal for the subsystem architect to change the parameters of the subsystem, although influencing the primary architect is well within bounds.

The subsystem architect is responsible for the overall design of a particular subsystem. He or she will solicit contributions from the engineering talent pool. The subsystem architect must work with the human resources group to ensure that technology talent continues to be available as the need arises. As you will see shortly, the engineering talent will be motivated to contribute to multiple subsystems if they wish to rise within the hierarchy. However, the subsystem architect must also create an environment where engineering talent is motivated to make such contributions. This is essential.

When it comes to new technology delivery, the subsystem architect must deliver a functional, quality system to the primary architect (or the next layer subsystem architect). The primary architect must have developed the trust and confidence to accept submissions with minimal reviews.

The subsystem architect also has responsibility to the release architect. Any issues with the subsystem will typically find their way through the release architect. The subsystem architect is highly motivated to work with the release architect to make the required enhancements and fixes to the currently released environment. Responsiveness will only improve the ongoing quality of the system.

There are a few key metrics you can put in place for the subsystem architect:

- **The ability to attract talent to the subsystem**—Also, by extension, you must do the work to ensure that talent is available.
- **The timely and quality submission of the subsystem**—The next level up in the hierarchy is the key input for this. If the submissions do not meet acceptable goals, then the subsystem architect should be replaced.
- **Innovation in the subsystem**—New technology and inventions need to happen at every layer in the overall system. Therefore, innovative technology needs to be measured every step of the way.
- **Succession planning**—While the primary and release architect form an interlocked disaster recovery system, subsystem architects will not necessarily have such a built-in system, but the good ones will. For the subsystem architect to climb to new heights within the hierarchy, a clear successor must be identified. The replacement, when it happens, should be a combined decision between the subsystem architect leaving the job and the next level in the hierarchy.

You should see a theme developing here. Rather than the organizational hierarchy being developed by top-down management decisions, a culture evolves that is based on the evolving maturity of the engineering talent and a clear desire to make contributions that enhance the quality and competitiveness of the overall system. Let's complete this theme with a look at the engineering talent.

Engineering Talent

The engineers in your organization are just that, talent. They are a valuable asset, not replaceable parts. When new to the organization, your talent needs time to adjust to the corporate culture, understand the system being developed, and decide the best place to make contributions. Different individuals will end up with a variety of goals. For some, it will be to climb to the highest level within the hierarchy; for others, it will be to make contributions as broadly as possible throughout the system to expand their knowledge as much as possible; and for others, it will be to stay peaked in one very specific area of the technology. You need to recognize the value of each one of these goals. They all add value to the system.

For an engineer to climb the hierarchy, he or she will need to demonstrate not only technological talent, but some degree of architectural vision, and maybe more importantly, significant interpersonal skills. These people skills will become more and more important the higher in the hierarchy the engineer aspires to reach.

The engineering talent needs to be measured on the quality, quantity, diversity, and innovation of their contributions. This combination of metrics create an interesting dynamic. If a favorite subsystem reaches a point of maturity, then the engineer must either innovate within the subsystem or move to another subsystem to make contributions. If the number of contributions becomes too low, then any number of material consequences can be established to reenergize the talent.

The key thing to watch for here is the number of rejected contributions. Since every level in the hierarchy is held accountable for a quality system, balanced with competitive functionality, bad contributions will be summarily rejected. Some rejections are normal and should be expected. It may simply imply a highly motivated engineer pushing the envelope. But, repeated and sustained rejections point to a problem with the talent that needs to be corrected.

The human resources group should continually enhance the engineering talent. We will look at the details of the human resources team a little later. Notice, however, the appendages on the engineering talent box. These represent other key parts of the larger organization. One of the key benefits of bazaar development is that everyone gets to play. While you must ensure that contributors have proper training on the system, the tools, and the rest of the infrastructure, your culture needs to encourage submissions from anywhere.

If other parts of your company have a desire to make contributions to enhance your system, you should look at this as a very positive development. First, it is an indicator that the current system is not meeting the needs of the users. Second, it provides additional talent that is highly motivated to make the system better than it is today. Contributions must still be accepted by one of the architects, and bad contributions should be rejected like any other. This will ensure that others within the company know that while they are encouraged to make contributions, only quality contributions that fit within the architectural constraints of the overall system will be accepted.

The other place that talent may come from is your external customers and partners. This falls under the special category of *gated communities*; we will look at these later in this chapter.

Human Resources

The open source community does not think too much about the management of human capital. There is no need to worry about things like deciding raises, issuing paychecks, making equipment available, or providing career counseling. This group is one of the key differences between bazaar development in the community and bazaar development in the corporation.

It is likely that the roles and responsibilities I describe here go far beyond what you would normally expect of your human resources group. This team plays a critical role. The goal of the technology team is to focus as much energy as possible on technology and product delivery. This implies that people management issues will take a peripheral role unless managed directly by another team. This is what the human resources group is all about.

People Development

Your talent needs to have resources available to help with career counseling and any number of professional development topics. It may be desirable to go to graduate school, or help with a specific development area, such as how to develop teams. In traditional companies, personal development will often be part of an employee's direct manager's responsibilities. In this style of development, direct management no longer exists, but there still needs to be a resource to help in personal development.

Overall corporate communications happen here as well. There needs to be a process for company management to communicate the overall company strategy to the employee population. While the engineering structure will ensure that the day-to-day work is aligned with the objectives of the technology being developed, corporate communications ensure that the employee has access to a larger strategic context.

Talent Management

This group is responsible for listening to the talent needs of the architects and ensuring that the required talent is available. If rare talent is needed, this is where the investment for acquisition needs to be focused. This team also ensures that there is diversity in the talent being sought. By diversity, I mean a mix of talent interested in specific technology areas, growing within a management hierarchy, and with varying degrees of people management skills.

This team must also play the "bad guy" role when it comes to how much talent the company can afford to have. This can sometimes be managed through a combination of permanent and temporary employees. But, if the company can no longer afford talent, this team must work with the engineering teams to help make the tradeoffs of which subsystems need more focus than others. At this point, the engineering teams can make choices such as shutting down contributions in a particular subsystem to ensure that the available talent is focused on the subsystems that need the most help. Recall that one of the measures for talent is the quantity of submissions. Talent that chooses to sit idle until a subsystem reopens for submission will suffer very negative consequences.

The other parts of talent management are ensuring that the best possible talent is available and always evolving the talent. This team needs to develop the processes that allow for the ongoing measurement of contributions by every engineer. They need to measure the ongoing rate of contributions, the diversity of the contributions, and the rejected contributions. Active processes need to be developed to proactively manage the situations where an individual is contributing at an unacceptable level. While this may seem harsh, this evolves into a self-selection system that makes it that those who can't make a useful contribution need to find a way, or find another home. Only your own individual corporate culture will determine the amount time an individual has to start making useful and sustained contributions.

Training

This team manages the combination of corporate training and engineering process training. Corporate training is the usual mix of vision, mission, and corporate goals along with identity and culture. Engineering process training gets the talent ready to submit contributions. While there can be some high-level training on the technology being developed, you should focus your energy on the tools and submission processes that the engineer can use. Most engineers tend to prefer some degree of trial by fire. Once they understand the processes used to submit contributions and their lifecycle, hands-on training and interacting with other engineers will rapidly start to deliver the rest.

Do not underestimate the need of the training team. If the engineers do not understand how to make productive contributions, everyone loses.

Testing and Integration

These are other functions you won't generally find in the open source community. The community's testing and integration schemes are often as simple as sending source files, patches, and fixes to the maintainer via email. More often, the set of tools described in Chapter 3 (CVS, Bugzilla, etc.) are the mainstay of the community. Testing largely happens by having a large user population running into difficulties during the development cycle. Note two extremes here. NASA will use up to 30 test engineers for each software developer, while the community will often have little formal testing. While it would be a stretch to assert that quality levels of open source software are on par with those of NASA, the track record speaks for itself. The real question is: Why is the community able to achieve such impressive quality results? Remember "given enough eye balls, all bugs are shallow"? This is what it boils down to.

In many corporations, access to a project's source code is carefully controlled and only those with an identified need-to-know are allowed to even look at the source; an even shorter list is allowed to modify the code. The culture you need to develop is one in which the more people that have access and can view the source, the better. Feedback on design, coding, and algorithms is always more than welcome. But, in the end, you need to release a product for commercial use; your user population counts on you for basic testing and quality. Since it is also likely that the size of the developer/user population in your organization is much smaller than the community at large, you will need more formal test and integration processes.

In Chapter 12, I will discuss the process of making your source available under an open source license. It is often impossible to predict when the time might come that you may want to do that. Therefore, from a source integration perspective, using the same tools as the community will give you the flexibility to integrate and potentially migrate to a community source base. In some cases, legacy or other company dynamics may force you into specific source integration systems. In these cases, take the opportunity to look at some of the commercial vendors that offer abstraction tools that allow you to work with both open source and traditional tools.

In all likelihood, you will need to retain much of your test infrastructure. If your new culture is working, you should see a dramatic decline in the problems found during test cycles. Experienced managers also understand that the purpose of the test team should not be to uncover defects, but rather to validate a working system.

Finance

Your colleagues on the finance team will also play a largely traditional role, but with a few notable exceptions. Because of your model of including participation from an ever-increasing population of talent, the cost structure models used in the business analysis will need to evolve. The finance team will also need to help balance the needs of the technology teams with the go-to-market teams and work with the human resources group to make sure the fixed cost structure associated with human talent is properly managed.

Market Planning

Another key role not generally found in the community at large is market planning. Recall that in the community, the developer is the user. This is a wonderful thing, but if you are delivering a product inside your company, or delivering a commercial product, you need a much better sense of user needs. In typical planning fashion, you will segment your markets and target them in an order of priority that yields the greatest return. This is where you have an advantage over community players. You can clearly scope the current and future target markets for the technology being developed for the primary architect. This information will provide far more guidance than the typical open source project tends to receive.

This team is also responsible for generating and calibrating the key metrics that make sure the team is focused on the right set of objectives. By measuring competitive performance, this provides direct feedback into how well the primary architect is doing his or her job. There is another positive side-effect that happens here. Many market planning teams want to plan products down to finite and individual features. As a result, engineering teams end up feeling as though they have no room left to innovate or add creativity. Since this team identifies the key markets, and the right competitive goals within these markets, the engineering teams have all the motivation they need to deliver the right technology with the right features.

Go-to-Market

So far in this discussion, I have been very careful to associate the technology team with technology delivery. This is because the responsibility for delivering a polished product is the responsibility of this team. To understand this concept, take a look at how the Linux operating system is delivered to the vast majority of customers. Linus works with a talented team to create a kernel. Thousands of other developers work to create and enhance what you now understand as the GNU system and other key software components. Then, a suite of distribution vendors combine all of these components and integrate them into a polished product for end-user consumption. What may not be so obvious is that each distribution vendor assembles the component parts differently, and adds custom tools and capability largely dependent on the market being targeted. As mentioned, some distribution vendors might target the server market, others the desktop, while still others real-time telecommunications applications.

This team fills the role equivalent to the distribution vendor. This can give you tremendous flexibility to take the same technology and deliver it to vastly different market segments. For smaller projects, you might have only one of these teams; for very large projects, you could have dozens. The management challenge will be to clearly draw the lines of where the technology team ends and the market teams begin. But, this does imply that you will need some engineering talent as part of your go-to-market teams. This talent can differ substantially from the core engineering teams.

This team is also responsible for completing all the elements of the value chain, including working with sales teams, manufacturing, support, and all the other organizational teams that are part of delivering a working solution to your customer, whether internal or external.

Other Structural Elements

The focus of this discussion has been largely on where engineering tends to occur within the organization, with some connection to the other teams immediately affected by such a fundamental change in development style. You will need to determine how any of the other structural connections are impacted. It will be important for you to communicate the changes to the support, manufacturing, sales, and other key partners of the organization. As an example, the support teams may welcome the ability to participate in the development and enhancement process and provide you with valuable customer input. There are other elements of development I did not cover here that you will need to assess based on your specific circumstances. For example, you may have a human factors team that needs to work with the engineering teams to ensure that accessibility and usability are well-covered in the product development cycle. Your key will be to maintain good communication throughout the organization.

Gated Communities

I quickly mentioned the notion of "gated communities" a little earlier in the chapter. As your culture evolves to welcome more and more participants to your development community, you will reach a point where your key customers and partners may want to join in the actual development process. While you cannot engage in a free-for-all that lets external partners modify the system, you can welcome this participation in a disciplined fashion.

Recall that the goal of this chapter is to expose you to the bazaar development process, not release your code to the public. "Gated communities" is the process of allowing customers and partners to engage in the development process, while keeping your source code proprietary.

Why allow customers and partners to participate in the development process? One of the key benefits of open source is the responsiveness that the community provides to identified problems. In the proprietary software world, many large customers get frustrated at their inability to get specific requests worked on. Some of these requests can be as simple as defect repairs, but they can also be sophisticated new feature enhancements. Partners are those companies that are dependent on your product for their products. Partner involvement also allows you to enhance your product. Therefore, your big win in gated communities is innovation that solves customer needs, and an opportunity to be responsive to customer issues by allowing direct involvement on their part.

The process of creating gated communities involves creating a network infrastructure that allows external parties access to the source base, but maintains strict security and privacy. You also need to build controls that identify the key partners that can participate.

You will need to establish confidential disclosure contracts with your partners. If you were able to build your source infrastructure based on open source conventions, you will find that your partners are able to join your community very effectively. You will also need to agree on IP ownership for any contributions made by your customers and partners. You should avoid situations where you cannot control IP. If you ever want to release your code under an open source license, you will want to make sure you have as few encumbrances as possible.

Finally, the next step will involve proper training, and some degree of relationship building between the engineers from customers and partners and the key engineers within your company.

Risks and Issues

Any new structure involves a degree of imperfection and some risks. This structure is no different. First, you need to translate this functional structure into a specific organizational structure. The choice of some of your key players will have a dramatic effect on the success of this model. In Chapter 13, we will go into more detail on the selection process of individuals within this model. There is also a transition risk as you attempt to move from whatever your current structure and model is to a new and different model. Ensuring that you have a detailed migration plan with detailed communications will be the key to minimizing this risk. You will also need to make a choice as to the right time in your release cycles to start implementing this new style of development. Also, if you use this as a guide for some of the key cultural goals, you can start an evolutionary process of encouraging open access to source within your organization.

I mentioned a few times the need to drive an open culture with few restrictions within the organization on the access to source code. While this is a requirement to apply an open source development model, since you are developing proprietary software, you still need to balance this openness with a need to know. You are still developing proprietary software, and you need to make sure that your IP is not transferred to other companies without your knowledge. The best way to manage this risk is to ensure that you have confidentiality agreements with your employees, and to never stop the education process to make sure your engineers clearly understand what they are doing.

Probably the biggest risk is the one associated with people management issues. Since this structure minimizes the role of direct management within the engineering ranks, you will want to ensure that counselors and coaches are readily available and that the human resources team is being proactive to make sure your engineering talent is a top priority.

Summary

This chapter covered a huge amount of ground in a very difficult and complex topic. You may even want to read through this chapter a few times. By demonstrating how the open source community would do development if it lived in the corporate world, you hopefully have received the dual benefit of understanding how the community accomplishes some of its amazing developments while being able to take some of the same techniques and applying them to your developments.

Before we extend your open source development knowledge into taking your source code public, we will take a detour through understanding the effects of open source on conventional business models, which will give you insight into why you will want to consider open sourcing some of your developments, as well as leveraging community work into your products and developments.

Value as a Function
of Time

Software vendors create technology in the hopes that more value will be created than the cost of developing the software. The more unique and significant the value, the more pricing power the vendor will have. The primary factors affecting pricing power are the value perceived by the customer and the competitive pressure in the market. Open source attacks pricing power in new ways and accelerates the devaluation of some technology. This chapter examines this new form of competition in the marketplace. Although this chapter is written with commercial software vendors in mind, it is equally useful for IT managers to understand how their vendors are being affected by market dynamics, and to also have visibility into new competitive offerings developing in the marketplace. Understanding the effect on resources is also important for IT managers. The objectives for this chapter are for you to understand:

- The economic impact of the time/value curve
- The effects of open source on the value of commercial software
- The effects of open source on the sustainability of value
- How to use the time/value effect to your advantage

As a developer of commercial software, you will need to accelerate your move up the value stack or risk seeing your value getting commoditized and no longer be in a position to generate enough revenue to recover your investment. To internalize the impact that open source software can have on your business, we will look at the market dynamics of another industry, which has been dealing with a similar effect for some time.

Pharmaceutical Industry

The pharmaceutical industry has been dealing with the devaluation of its products on fixed time schedules for years. In the mid-1980s, I started to suffer from a mild stomach irritation. Over a period of about 18 months, the irritation gradually made my days more and more unpleasant every time I ate. It took a number of attempts on the part of doctors, over many months, to diagnose the problem. While there was no cure, my irritation could be treated by using medication to reduce the production of acid in my stomach. Unfortunately, I reacted negatively to the medication that was commonly prescribed at the time. A fairly new drug, called Ranitidine, had recently become available. You might now recognize this drug under the brand name Zantac. I will get back to this brand recognition a little bit later. After using this new drug for about a week, I was symptom-free. Eighteen months of feeling sick almost every day were finally over. I would have been willing to pay anything for Zantac. In my book, it was a wonder drug. Fortunately, I had very good insurance. I was consuming 1200mg of Zantac every day. At about $1.80 for each 150mg pill, my regimen cost almost $15/day, or well over $5000/year. Since any other medication normally used at the time actually made my condition worse, the insurance company had no alternative but to pay for this specific treatment. There was no competition for Ranitidine. I ended up taking Zantac for about seven years and I am now embarrassed to admit that my final cure was to quit smoking.

When I did a recent online check for Ranitidine, I found I could get it for about $0.12 cents for a 150mg pill. My $35,000, seven-year treatment today would cost less than $2,500, about a 93% reduction. How would you like to have your product devalued at that rate? The cause of this dramatic price change is the availability of a generic version of Ranitidine. Generic drugs become available shortly after the original developer's patent expires. For big drugs, it usually happens on the very day the patent expires. I will extend this comparison to demonstrate how the pharmaceutical industry must recover its costs and adjust its business models. Then, I will transition back to the specifics of the software industry and apply this new paradigm.

Cost, Value, Return, and Time

The pharmaceutical industry has the very distinct benefit of knowing exactly when its patent expiration will have the effect of having generic versions of drugs begin to appear in the market. This allows the industry to build well-understood cost/return models. Take a look at the chart in Figure 10–1.

This chart depicts a simplified view of the economic lifecycle of new drug development. My goal is not to make you an expert in the economic models of this industry, but to use this to parallel the effects of open source on the software industry.

Pharmaceutical companies invest large amounts of money in research for new drugs. Their goal is to discover new treatment options for any number of ailments that our society must contend with. The major motivation for these companies to incur high research costs is the knowledge that their discoveries will be protected by applying for a patent, and if that patent is awarded, exclusive rights to the drug for a period of 20 years (there are cases when the life of a patent can be extended).

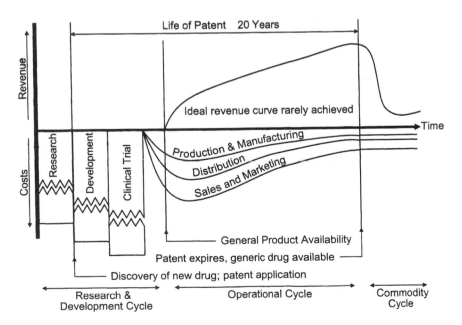

Figure 10–1   Economic return model for prescription drugs.

At some point in the research cycle of this simplified model, a discovery for a new drug occurs. To protect the discovery, the company will apply for a patent (patents take 2–4 years to be awarded). The next stage is to do a number of developments based on the new discovery. The development cycle includes refining the drug, testing the effects on a variety of non-human subjects, and looking for compound activity against the target disease.

The development cycle will next evolve to clinical trials. This stage involves controlled testing with human subjects. The drug compound is tested for safety, efficacy, and ideal dosage. Even before approval is received from regulatory agencies, if the new drug compound appears promising, the production cycle will begin. The product can be made available for sale only after the drug has completed clinical trials and has been approved by regulatory agencies. In some cases, the compound will not be approved and the production process will need to be halted. Note that by the time a drug reaches the market, the patent's clock has been ticking for years. The goal for the drug company is to make it through development and trials and get approval in the shortest possible time, while ensuring delivery of a safe product.

Even before a drug gets full regulatory approval, drug companies will start to ramp up their production capabilities, train their sales forces, and start seeding the market for their great new product. Then the operational cycle begins. During this cycle, the goal is to maximize the revenue for the new product. The product must not only cover the operational costs of manufacturing, sales, marketing, and distribution, it must also be able to recover the costs of the research and development cycle. If the revenue for the drug exceeds the ongoing operational costs as well as the research and development costs, only then will the drug reach a positive return on investment (ROI).

A complexity not shown in the diagram is that at any one time, there will be research underway in a number of different areas. Some research will never turn into a product. In fact, most compounds never reach the market. Therefore, not only must a new drug cover its own costs, but it must also contribute to recover the costs of inevitable failed research attempts. The revenue combination of all drugs currently released in the market must generate enough operational cash flow to fund ongoing research and return a profit to investors.

One clear advantage that the pharmaceutical industry has is a clear view of when a patent will expire. Therefore, it knows when a product will be commoditized by a generic drug. Therefore, the industry can build very accurate cost models that allow it to balance a price that the market will bear with all the operational costs and ensure a positive ROI and acceptable operational profit. This ability to predict when the value will be commoditized also allows the industry to begin the cycle of reducing operational costs at exactly the right time. This overall predictability allows for a very efficient and accurate cost model, even if there is a degree of uncertainty in how much research will turn into revenue-producing products.

Recovering from Commodity

What will happen when a generic drug becomes available and the market will no longer pay a premium price for the drug? The drug company must develop a new business model to sustain profitability with this newfound competition. You will note from the chart that revenue did not reach zero. There are a number of reasons why there is a continued revenue stream:

- Brand awareness for the product by individuals, pharmacies, and doctors
- Trust in the company delivering the drug
- Perceived and real quality and consistency of the premium product
- Adverse effects in some patients of the inert components in the generic drug
- The belief by some that drug companies should continue to be rewarded for their research efforts and ongoing contributions through innovation

These reasons are why drug companies can continue to charge a small premium for their product even though a generic drug (or commodity product) is also available. Recall from the earlier discussion that the generic drug will force significant price decreases. Depending on the specific circumstance, the company may choose to reduce the price of their product so that the premium above the generic is much smaller than before the patent expired.

The other way to maintain higher revenues for a product is to develop new business models or find new applications. For some medicines, this may mean expansion into other global regions or combining medications in innovative ways to treat new ailments. Recall my earlier discussion on Ranitidine and the brand name Zantac. The reason you are probably familiar with Zantac is because GlaxoSmithKline, the drug's creator, developed a low-dosage version (Zantac 75) of their product that was approved for over-the-counter sale. The industry refers to this scenario as an "Rx to OTC (over-the-counter) switch." Through the use of extensive advertising, Zantac has become a very successful and popular antacid treatment for millions of individuals. Even though generic versions of Ranitidine are available with a prescription, brand power and a non-prescription version continue to provide a revenue source for the drug's developer.

This is the type of creative business model evolution that the software industry must develop to maintain profitability when open source software becomes an alternative for customers.

Open Source Effect on Software

What do my stomach ailments have to do with software and open source? While there are some key differences, the open source effect on the commercial software industry is very similar to the generic drug effect on the pharmaceutical industry. The pharmaceutical industry has been dealing with this phenomenon for many years and has learned to fine-tune their business models accordingly. This is a new phenomenon for the software industry and we are all still learning to adapt to the effect.

Let me take a look at some of the key differences between the two industries. A software product usually contains a long list of features and capabilities, while a drug is usually a finite compound. It is generally easier to patent an invention where the embodiment of that invention is a finite compound than it is to patent a whole software product. This is due to the fact that the software patent will likely apply to an invention that is embodied in a small subset (or feature) of the whole software product. There are many in the open source community who object entirely to the whole notion of software patents. These objections stem from the fact that the community freely gives away its IP and expects the same in return. Even if a method has been patented, defending that software patent can be expensive. Since the software industry is so dynamic and broad, it is not possible to verify that absolutely no prior art exists when awarding a patent. This means that even if a particular software method has been patented, you may find prior art when attempting to defend that patent. Software patents also hold for 20 years.

A generic drug will generally attempt to be identical to the premium product. Competing software products, even if the competition is open source, will generally have very different models to accomplish the same task. The end result is that while the drug companies can count on a degree of exclusivity for a number of years, it is rare for a software company to maintain any exclusivity in a particular product category.

Predictability is also very different in the two models. While the drug industry can build fairly accurate cost models around a predictable product life, the software industry never knows when a competitor will provide a better product, or a lower cost alternative. The drug industry must still contend with other competitive pressures similar to the software industry, and therefore, revenue profiles always involve risk. Figure 10–2 replicates the earlier model, but this time as a software-based economic model.

The open source community is motivated to produce software that has the widest possible appeal. What this means is that if you are in a niche market, the number of open source developers available to commoditize your product are greatly reduced, although not eliminated. Some of the first open source products developed were Web servers, database engines, desktop interfaces, and programming tools. However, there are a number of specialized products and applications for which there is no open source equivalent. The key here is that the more broadly applicable the software product, the more likely it is for an open source equivalent to become available.

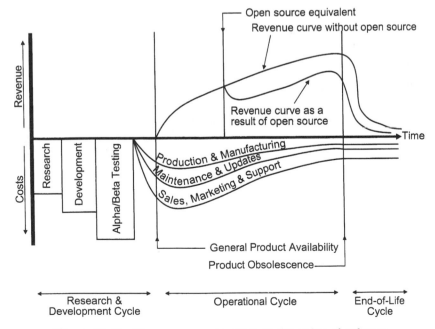

Figure 10–2 The open source effect on the value of software.

You should also be very careful about believing that because you are in a small niche industry, you will not be at risk of the effects of open source software. One example is photo finishing and film production. The open source community has created a very advanced photo editing product called GIMP (GNU image manipulation program), and this product is being expanded for film editing. While GIMP and its film editing counterpart may not meet every user's requirements, it is a clear leading indicator of things to come and hint that the value you may be delivering will soon come under significant price pressures. Ironically, commercial products now seem to be borrowing from GIMP!

Figure 10–2 depicts the effects of open source on the value of software and the power of commercial vendors to command a premium price for that value. Almost any commercial software has value. Over time, it is normal that the value of the software decreases in the eyes of the customer. The devaluation comes from competitive forces and a somewhat natural commodity effect. Twenty years ago, the power windows on your car were an expensive add-on option. Today, you would likely be very surprised if they were not included in a base vehicle. Software vendors (and auto-makers) typically respond to this natural devaluation process by continuously adding new features and new capabilities. These updates refresh the value on an ongoing basis. When it comes to enterprise software, vendors can maintain value by being the only entity with the ability to support the software for customers. Another factor that will protect enterprise software vendors is barrier to entry. Once a customer has committed to a particular software choice, as long as the ongoing cost of support and updates is less than the cost of replacement, the vendor can continue to charge a premium.

Open source has the effect of accelerating devaluation in a number of dimensions. First, since in many cases a large number of developers will attack the problem, the time required to create a comparable offering to yours can be greatly reduced. Second, since the community is generally not motivated by money, features for which you would charge a premium are all included at no charge. Third, although a barrier to entry will always be maintained, since the license cost of the open source software is usually zero, that barrier will be dramatically reduced. That final barrier is usually tied to some form of support availability. The size of the barrier will depend on the end-user's willingness to engage in open source support models.

The final challenge is predictability. The pharmaceutical industry can predict with a high degree of accuracy when its products will be commoditized and it can react with adjusted cost models at just the right point in the lifecycle. The open source effect is much less predictable. First, if you don't pay attention to community efforts currently underway, you can be surprised by an open source version of your product. Second, since software products are usually an amalgamation of features and capabilities, it is difficult to predict when an open source product will reach the threshold of "good enough" in the majority of customers' minds.

Devaluation as a Competitive Advantage

The key to benefiting from open source is to understand how to take advantage of devaluation, and the community rather than to react in a defensive way. Here are some examples of defensive reactions to open source:

- **Aggressive patent use**—Some software companies will respond with patent attacks on the open source community. This is not an advisable tactic. Since the community has limited resources to defend itself in the courtroom from patent attacks, it will usually respond by sustained and aggressive negative public relations attacks. In almost all cases, it will be possible to write code that does not infringe the patent claim and therefore little will be gained in the end. Unisys started to enforce a patent that covered the compression algorithm used for Graphics Interchange Format (GIF) files, which was commonly used for images on the Internet. The community responded by simply using JPEG or PNG files instead.
- **Monolithic software**—Most software today is written as a collection of functional layers, each building on one another. Open source software developers typically begin their projects at the lowest layer in any given software stack. By creating monolithic software, vendors hope to prevent commoditization from the bottom of the stack. However, the effect will usually be to have the community create a better architected software solution and commoditize the monolithic software all at once.
- **Competition**—One common reaction is to attempt to compete with the open source community. This is usually a knee-jerk reaction that will go away with time. Competing against a community of first-rate developers who are not motivated by profit or constrained by time is a foolhardy exercise. At some point, usually sooner than you think, time and resources will make such a move impossible to sustain.

The best option is to participate proactively with the open source community and use devaluation to your advantage. In the next chapter, we will examine a number of business model alternatives. For now, focus on the mindset and cultural attitude you need to develop to work with the community with a positive attitude and look at this eventuality as a good thing.

Even without the open source effect, there will be a natural devaluation of your technology that occurs over time. However, your need to sustain the technology so it can continue to support new value up the software stack is also a drain on resources. The end result is that you continue to apply resources on technology that your customers have long since considered base functionality for which they would not pay extra.

All software companies have a finite set of resources. In most cases, companies continuously struggle with being able to apply resources on capabilities higher up the value stack. The trick is to partner with the community to supplement resources lower in the software stack so that you can deploy your resources to create capabilities that generate more value and return to the company. Figure 10–3 shows you how your resources should be aligned with the value you deliver to your customer.

Your goal should be to allocate your resources as high up the value stack as you possibly can. The next chapter will give you the details on how to combine your proprietary software with open source software so that you can make the right choices on resource reallocation. A key thing to note here is that even at the lowest part of the software stack, you

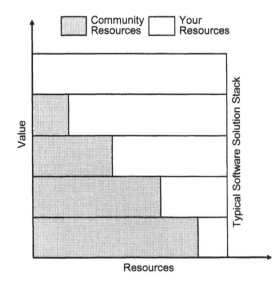

Figure 10–3   Resource allocation correlated to value delivery.

should still allocate some of your resources. You should never adopt a mindset that you can simply "dump" software to the community and it will take care of itself. Someone in your organization will need to keep the project going, focus community efforts, and make sure that the lowest levels of the software stack continue to meet the requirements of the components at the top of the stack. You will likely want to make sure that your company retains the role of maintainer even at this level of the stack.

The other advantage of maintaining this close connection with the community at every level in the software stack is that you get an inside view of when, where, and how the value you deliver is being affected by community developments. This will give you a host of leading indicators that you can monitor and react to accordingly.

Value Stuck in Time

At a recent LinuxWorld event, I went for drinks with Tim O'Reilly (of O'Reilly Books). We talked about a number of different open source topics and I used the phrase "value as a function of time." After I described the concept, he enlightened me with a very different view of what the concept might mean. His view was that the open source community is not beholden to a timeframe to deliver a useful and capable product. Anyone who has lived in the high-technology industry for any length of time will be well-aware of situations where products are released before their time. When these situations occur, the product is often shelved and never again sees the light of day. The free software community doesn't have such restrictions and technology can find new uses when the community is finally ready for it. After our meeting, I started to think a bit more about this concept that Tim had brought forward and realized that this concept of value stuck in time had already happened to me.

Pilot Foundation Classes

In 1996, USRobotics released a revolutionary PDA called the Pilot 5000. Today, most of you will be familiar with the descendants of that device as the Palm family of PDAs (many still call it the PalmPilot). I was so excited with this device that not only did I get one, I immediately wanted to start programming applications for it. The operating system for the Pilot (now called PalmOS) was based on a C language API. I was an object-oriented programmer and really wanted to write for the device using C++. While this was technically possible, it would only be effective if I could use the PalmOS API as a collection of object-oriented C++ class libraries. What I needed to do was a much smaller equivalent of what Microsoft had done to build their Microsoft Foundation Classes (MFC). The MFC was a set of class libraries that dramatically increased the efficiency of writing applications for Windows by encapsulating the operating system's Win32 API.

I ended up writing what I called the Pilot Foundation Classes. It was a part-time project that I usually worked on only during transatlantic business trips. Although I completed most of my project, another developer beat me to it and released a similar project. There was no reason for me to compete with his offering. I had learned quite a bit about the PalmOS platform and I was still very happy with the time I had spent on development. It turns out my experience in building foundation classes to encapsulate an operating system interface would not go to waste.

Jump

One of the key contributors to the Palm (then Pilot) ecosystem was a developer named Greg Hewgill. Greg had already delivered an impressive emulator called CoPilot that was the mainstay of every developer's tool suite (I will come back to this emulator as an example of an open source business model in the next chapter). Around 1997, Greg started to work on a different project he called Jump. Although the "official" definition of Jump is an acronym for Java User Module for Pilot, Greg actually claims it came from listening to the popular Van Halen song of the same name during a late-night hacking session. Jump allowed a developer to write Java code and then use Jump to translate it into the low-level machine language used by Palm devices. (Those familiar with Java will know that Java code normally runs inside a virtual machine known as a Java virtual machine, or JVM. Jump translated Java code directly into Motorola 68K assembly code and attached a runtime garbage collector to the application.) While Greg was releasing beta versions of Jump, I was creating a demonstration application called the "WorldClock." (I later renamed WorldClock to DeskClock; it is shown in Figure 10–4). It was a simple application that displayed three different time zones simultaneously on the display. The plan was for Greg to include my demonstration applications when Jump finally released as a training aid for new Jump developers.

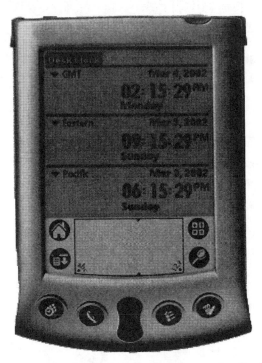

Figure 10–4   The PalmOS emulator running the DeskClock.

This is also where my new skills in creating foundation classes came back to life. Java is an object-oriented language, and creating a foundation class for the PalmOS API in Java was the next natural step. A few of us started working on PilotJFC (Pilot Java Foundation Classes), but this time, it was a bit more of a community effort. This is one example of technology I had developed that ended up being reused in a way I would have never predicted.

Although I never found out why, Greg eventually stopped working on Jump. There were some significant limitations in Jump that made it difficult to continue to use as a development platform. Gradually, the community that had formed around Jump dispersed. Greg conceded that since he was not working on Jump anymore, he should release the source so that others could continue his work. He did release Jump under the GNU GPL. I eventually stopped reading the newsgroups and lost touch. Unbeknownst to me, a few years later, a developer by the name of Ralph Kleberhoff re-ignited the Jump project as Jump2.

You can imagine my astonishment when nearly four years after I had stopped any development, on February 27, 2001, I (and another JFC developer) received the following email from Jim Birchfield:

From: Jim Birchfield
Sent: Tuesday, February 27, 2001 1:35 PM
To: Martin Fink
Subject: PilotJFC Resurrection

```
I have recently started using Jump for an application and
was pointed to some older postings concerning PilotJFC by
Noli.

I have since taken the version of JFC I was given and
brought it up to speed with the latest version of Jump. I
have also finished porting the WorldClock over to this new
architecture. Along the way I have made some changes and
enhancements, but all in all it was pretty sound when I
got it.

Could either of you tell me the status of PilotJFC as far
as either of you are concerned. I would like to add it as
an 'extra' on top of the Jump distribution. I am offering
to take over the development and upkeep of it. But I don't
want multiple versions floating around and splintering.

So, what I would like to do is take over the code, making
sure you guys are mentioned in the credits, create some
more demos, and turn it into an official part of Jump.

Comments guys?
```

Tim O'Reilly made me think about something I had already experienced. Software that had been developed by a number of individuals "sat on a shelf" until there was a need from the user community. This demonstration should be an incentive for you to actively participate in the community in areas related to your software interests. Even if developments are stalled, or moving at a very slow pace, do not ignore them. All it takes is a motivated developer to re-ignite the activity and have an open source product become readily available. In some cases, you may be the one who is best motivated to accelerate the project.

As a side note, notice a few things about Jim's email. First, he asked the original authors before "taking" their work. Second, he assured me he would give due credit for other's work. Third, note that he uses the word "distribution" in the same way I described for non-Linux distributions in Chapter 5. Finally, Jim does not want to compete with other efforts in the community. This one, short email exemplifies the very culture of the open source community.

Summary

This chapter was a demonstration of the economic impact that open source software can have on your product. Your choice in responding to this economic effect can be to attack, be defensive, or even try to compete. Your best option will always be to participate and partner with the community as an opportunity to refocus your resources to tasks that will yield much greater value and return to your company. IT managers can also benefit from this effect by expanding their available resources to accelerate IT projects.

You also saw that participating actively in the community would allow you to keep track of projects, even stalled ones, and plan your business model evolution in a more predictable way.

Now that you can see the economic effects and your best response, it is time to understand how your business model can and should evolve. The next chapter goes into the detail of business models so that you can take the best possible advantage of open source.

Business Models—
Making Money

As a developer of software products, there will undoubtedly come a time when you will recognize that Linux and open source are having a direct effect on your revenue stream. You will need to do something to adjust how you develop products and look at your revenue sources in a different way. As you learn about Linux and open source, and the concept of free software, you will then need to understand how you can make money with a new product, service, and support paradigm. This chapter will look at a number of different business models and the different options that are available to you. While every business is different, if you read through each of these models, you should be able to adapt one or more of them to your specific situation. Your goal for this chapter is to understand the variety of different business models and use this information as a guide to adapt your business accordingly.

While this chapter is written with software product companies in mind, it is also useful for IT managers to be aware of the challenges facing their software vendors. A change in a business model by software vendors will invariably alter purchasing processes for the IT manager. Here is the list of the most common open source business models that we will examine throughout this chapter:

- Commercial software for Linux
- Services and support tied to an open source product
- Enhancing commercial products with open source software

- Open source software to enable hardware components
- Commercializing open source through dual-licensing
- Lowering the cost of end-of-life
- Building an ecosystem

The free software movement and many in the open source community believe that software in all its forms should be free. While this reference is always meant to imply freedom of access to the source code, in most cases, it will also imply software without license fees. This chapter does **not** attempt to present a case that all software should be without cost, rather that very successful business models can be established using open source as an additional component of your business. Open source can be a very good thing for your business if you understand how to integrate it properly into your existing product and services portfolio.

This chapter will examine the details of business model opportunities. In the next chapter, we will examine the processes involved in either using open source within your products or releasing open source software to the community.

Know Your Value

The most fundamental assessment you need to make before examining open source business models is to be clear about your core business. Who are your customers and what value are you trying to deliver to them? You learned in the previous chapter than any value gets commoditized over time. Open source has the effect of accelerating the commodity effect of the value you are trying to deliver. Your goal is to continually deliver more and higher value to your customers. This implies that components you deliver lower in the stack are not components for which your customers are willing to pay as much as they were willing to in the past.

If you are clear about your value proposition to your customers, then you can easily let go of components that are required for your business and must be delivered, but for which you cannot count on for any more revenue. This is where open source will have a positive effect on your business. By leveraging the community at large, you can focus your investments higher up in the value stack.

This process can be very disconcerting to managers within your organization. It implies that value they have successfully delivered in the past will now come from other sources. The cultural shift you must undertake is to help your managers and their employees continuously make the shift to higher value contributions, while rewarding strong participation in the open source community.

Assuming you clearly understand your business strategy and the differentiated value you deliver to your customers, there are a number of business model alternatives that you can begin to weave into your existing business.

Commercial Software and Linux

This is the most simplistic business model, but the point must still be made. There are many individuals who believe that you cannot sell or run commercial, proprietary software on the Linux operating system. With very few exceptions, proprietary application software can be packaged and sold for Linux in the same way as you would package and sell your application for any other operating system. There are many examples of proprietary application software available today for Linux and nothing in the Linux license (the GPL) requires the proprietary code to be published. Figure 11–1 is a view of a regular application running on Linux as well as a kernel-intrusive application running on Linux.

There may be instances where your commercial application crosses the kernel boundaries within Linux (i.e., a portion of your application software runs within the kernel). In this very specific instance, you will need to manage the process of building and packaging your application differently, and make a few business decisions. Since the Linux kernel is licensed under the GPL, the portions of your application that integrate with the kernel must also be licensed under the GPL. Review Chapters 2 and 3 for the discussion on kernel modules and the GPL for more specific details.

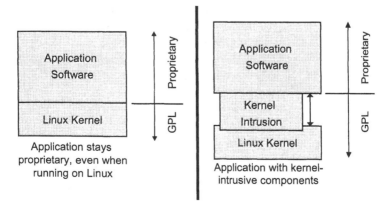

Figure 11–1   Commercial software running on Linux.

If you understand the value you deliver to your customer, you will likely accept that the kernel-intrusive components of your software are not where your customers derive value. If your business cannot accept releasing any of your software under the GPL, and your application is kernel-intrusive, then you will not be able to release it for use with Linux. You learned in Chapter 2 that it is possible to create proprietary kernel modules. Since this practice is not recommended, I assume that this option is not available. If you have well-defined interfaces between the portions of your software that are kernel-intrusive and the portions that are not, you will be able to release your software without any difficulty.

The kernel-intrusive components of your application software will be delivered either as modules or patches to the Linux kernel. You can then aggregate these GPL components with the proprietary portions of your application and package and deliver the solution to your customer.

Support and Services Tied to Open Source

Linux distribution vendors created one of the first business models used in the open source community. The most basic form of this model sets out to sell support for the distribution a vendor provides. Most Linux distributions contain only open source software. Since vendors package their distributions with open source components they have developed, they are the experts on the package. With these open source distributions, a number of business models have developed:

- **Retail packaging**—Many customers are willing to pay for the simple convenience of media and manuals. Most are still unaware that they can simply download or copy the software legally and at no cost. Many Linux distributions are available at retail.
- **Support**—Distribution vendors typically bundle support services with their retail packages to help customers with installation and any other difficulties they may encounter. Large corporate customers will purchase comprehensive support services for their complex installations. Some companies, such as LinuxCare, are dedicated to support services for a broad range of open source offerings.
- **Subscriptions**—This is part of the services portfolio offered by some distribution vendors. Subscription services offer a number of options for keeping your software automatically up-to-date. Ximian Corporation uses subscription services to provide update services to users of the GNOME desktop.

- **Brand associations**—Hardware and software vendors may work with distributions to associate them with their brand through bundling and other business activities. Depending on the situation, the vendor may charge for this association. The association will usually imply some form of certification, which may be important to some customers.
- **Professional services**—By continuously developing a distribution, vendors can use it as a "calling card" to demonstrate their core competence. Red Hat specializes in providing professional services associated with its Linux brand.

To use these business models, you must do some fundamental business case analysis that measures the costs of developing the "calling card" (in this case, a full distribution), and the revenue associated with each of the opportunities in the above list. Many companies are discovering that sustaining a business this way is difficult and are supplementing their business model with more traditional methods such as reselling proprietary licensed software.

Aggregating and Enhancing

This business model option usually involves combining open source software with proprietary software to provide a more complete solution to customers. In some cases, it may combine open source software with a proprietary hardware product (I discuss the hardware business model later in this chapter); but in many cases, you can enhance your proprietary software product by incorporating open source components. In other cases, you can add proprietary functionality to an existing open source offering and sell the enhanced package. Figure 11–2 shows how you can aggregate an open source application with proprietary components to sell as a complete solution to your customer.

A good example of this business model in action is a product from Covalent Technologies. The Apache Web Server is the most used Web server on the Internet and is *the* open source "killer application." Covalent Technologies starts with this open source Web server technology and adds enterprise class capabilities needed by large corporations. Covalent adds manageability, security, and resiliency enhancements to make the most used Web server platform ready for commercial deployment. Covalent also provides support services for large customers. Since the management team is involved in the development of the Apache Web Server,

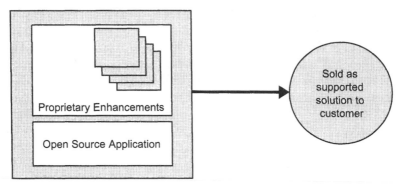

Figure 11–2 Enhancing open source with proprietary software.

this close connection between the open source community and commercial deployment provides an ideal bridge for customers.

It is possible for any number of companies to build new, commercial functionality on top of the Apache Web Server platform, and even compete while doing it. If it is done right, each of the competing companies will actually work together to make the core Apache Web Server as good as it can be, while competing on the value-added functionality on top of the server. Each company will understand that the value they deliver to their customers is not in the Web server, but rather in the tools and the support they deliver above and beyond the server.

This business model can be repeated with any number of core open source platforms such as Internet servers, clustering technologies, file systems, user interfaces, graphics art tools, etc. The list goes on and on. You can focus on delivering very attractive value while not getting caught up in the low-level components that are required and for which customers are not willing to invest.

Commercializing with a Dual-License

I briefly introduced the concept of dual-licensing in Chapter 3 using the ReiserFS file system as one example. This section covers it under the context of a business model. This particular model requires copyright ownership, or an acceptable license, for the source code. Using dual-licenses implies that you are maintaining an open source (usually GPL) version of the software, and also releasing a version of the same software under a commercial license. The business model revolves around traditional software licenses and support revenues for the commercial version of the software. This model will often involve some differences between the open source version and a proprietary commercial version. Differences will usually take the form of newer software, more tested software, or software enhancements not available with the open source version. This model may also include a time component. This means that open source releases may happen many months after the commercial release. Figure 11–3 is a more complete picture than the one presented in Chapter 3 to demonstrate this model.

Among the benefits of this business model are the ability to take advantage of the community of developers interested in your product and the opportunity to lower your development costs. The open source version can also create a large user population that increases awareness of your product. Although the commercial version of the product may differ from the open source version, the community wins by having access to an open source version of the software. While there will be some revenue loss due to some customers only using the open source version of the software, the increased user base and awareness will often result in expanding your customer base.

To execute this model, you must release all or portions of your application software under an open source license. The next chapter will outline the process you need to follow to ensure that you can do the release, which will require that you are the copyright owner (or have the required license) for all parts of the software. Your company will take on the role of maintainer for the GPL release of the software. As the maintainer, you

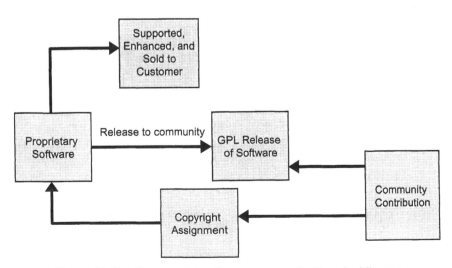

Figure 11–3   Commercial software managed with a dual-license.

have the choice to accept or reject contributions to the source tree. You can therefore request a copyright assignment as part of the contribution. What this means is that every developer who makes a contribution will also assign the copyright for the contribution to your company. Appendix B contains an example of a copyright assignment. However, you should always seek legal council to ensure you comply with all local laws. Copyright assignment usually allows the copyright owner to re-release the software under a proprietary license as well as an open source license. Also, if you own the copyright, you can freely mix the software with any other proprietary code you might own.

You should be careful with both the dual-licensing method and seeking copyright assignment. Depending on the project, the community may object to copyright assignment. Make sure you seek council with potential members of your community before assuming that everyone will agree to assign you their copyright.

Hardware

One of the easiest business models to understand and work with is the hardware business model. This model assumes that the value you deliver to your customer is derived from the hardware. The hardware you deliver will typically be some type of peripheral device or some type of interface hardware to a peripheral device. Examples of peripheral devices are printers, scanners, and disk drives. Examples of interface hardware are video cards, disk controllers, and bus interfaces that implement the Universal Serial Bus (USB) standard.

When delivering hardware is your primary objective, you will generally assume that the more places you can enable your device to function, the greater your potential market. Working with the open source community to deliver device drivers (the software interfaces between devices and the operating system) can be one of the most effective ways for your company to expand your potential market at a very low cost.

The hardware business model is predicated on your ability to define a clear separation between the ability to control the hardware and using of the hardware functionality.

Separate Device Interface from Device Functionality

The best way to explain this is through a real example. Imagine you are selling interface hardware to allow consumers to watch television on their computers. Your hardware will likely be some form of interface card that is inserted in the computer with connectors for the incoming television signal. In this example, there are two primary software components that you would deliver to your customer: the device driver that controls the interface card and the television viewing software. Your business model questions should be:

- Does my customer perceive the device driver's value?
- Does my customer perceive the television viewing software's value?

To take advantage of the open source community and increase your potential market, you must answer "No" to the first question and either "Yes" or "No" to the second. Figure 11–4 depicts the interconnection between the application software, the device driver, and the hardware interface.

By answering "No" to the first question, you acknowledge that enabling your hardware on the broadest set of platforms enhances your market position. Your next goal should be to work in close partnership with the community to enable and encourage it to implement on that broad array of platforms for you. As I mentioned in the previous chapter, you need to maintain some resources on the project that can act as your conduit with the community. If you are working cooperatively with the community, it will generally do most of the development work for you. You can accelerate the development cycle and enhance your relationship by donating some of your hardware to key members of the community

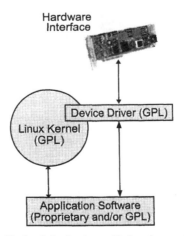

Figure 11–4 Interfacing with hardware devices.

who have a solid track record of developing device drivers. If your cost on a hardware device is only a few hundred dollars, it is a very good bargain in return for sophisticated development work.

You must also decide the degree of control you would like to maintain over the device driver. The implication of this decision is in how you would like to maintain and support the driver. You may be able to find a developer in the community who would like to take the lead in developing the driver, and therefore be its maintainer. Alternatively, you may choose to maintain the driver within your company. The choice is yours and will be based on the costs you are willing to incur versus the control you wish to maintain. Even if you make the choice to develop and maintain the driver within your company, the community is still free to develop its own version if it believes it can do a better job or expose more functionality. A collaborative relationship with the community will usually ensure that both parties do the right thing and avoid duplicate developments.

Even though you now have a device driver to link the television interface to the operating system, you still do not have a useful solution for the end-user. What you need now is software that allows the user to watch television, change channels, adjust the volume, and all the other normal television viewing functions. More exotic solutions would allow the user to record television shows, display station names, or even skip commercials. If the hardware is compelling and the device driver has been written, it is highly likely that creative developers in the community will develop any number of solutions. Even if the community creates compelling solutions for your hardware, it is also possible for you to develop even better capabilities as proprietary and supported software. Your choice will be based on your ability to derive additional revenue from the proprietary solution and your desire to deliver a fully supported customer experience. Figure 11–4 depicts how the driver itself is GPL and developed with the community, but that the higher value functionality can be available from either the open source community or delivered as a proprietary solution.

Open Documentation to the Hardware Interface

For a community of developers to be successful in developing device drivers for your hardware, they will usually need good documentation about the functional aspects of your hardware. There are many examples of reverse engineering by the community; however, it makes much more sense to give the community enough information to do the work so they can do it right and your hardware does not get commoditized. The release of documentation on the internal capabilities of the product tends to cause tremendous heartache for many managers. You will rarely need to release the complete documentation set that covers the entire functionality of your hardware. What you will need to release is enough documentation so that a developer can control the device or interface hardware.

The best way to accomplish this is to develop the engineering processes that define a new class of documentation. This documentation releases the interface specifications, without releasing proprietary data that would help your competitors. In some extreme cases, it may affect the actual design of the hardware.

In some cases, you will be sourcing components of the end hardware product from third parties, often referred to as OEMs. In these cases, you must negotiate up front with your OEMs for the proper documentation that you can release to the community for the development of device drivers. In some cases, you may be able to negotiate with the OEM to develop the device driver or manage that process with the open source community.

As an alternative to releasing formal documentation, you can develop a reference device driver and release it to the open source community. The community can use this reference driver as a starting point, and as a surrogate for hardware documentation.

Bundling with Hardware

The final aspect of the hardware business model is to include open source software with your hardware, or resell hardware with an open source solution. The goal in either case is to give the perception of delivering extra value or a more complete solution to the customer. You must consider the support implications of bundling an open source software solution with your hardware.

End-of–Life Model

The end-of-life business model requires a complex analysis that balances goals of lowering costs, accelerating the end-of-life, and understanding the effects of enabling a self-sustaining community.

When a company ends the life of a product, it must consider the effects on its customer base. Customers who have made an investment to deploy a product do not usually respond well to having their investment made obsolete. Companies ending the life of a product must consider the negative impact on their image within their customer base. While customers will often understand the logic behind terminating the life of a product, they will still be angry about the need to develop an alternate solution and incur the costs of the change.

If you end the life of a product, you will generally offer a support life for many years to build goodwill with your customers and give them ample time to decide how to migrate to a new solution. During this support lifecycle, you will assign engineers who can continue to respond to customer issues and fix any new defects that may be encountered. While customers will generally be willing to pay for this support, you are incurring costs and defocusing your energy on something that is obviously no longer strategic.

In these cases, open source can be an effective tool to build goodwill with your customers, lower your internal support costs, and ensure that you are focused on the strategic direction of the company. If your core business model is not usually tied to support, open source can also be an effective way to work with other companies who specialize in providing support for open source products. It will often be possible to create an environment where customers band together to continue supporting and enhancing the solution on their own.

If you are exiting the class of business for which you are doing an end-of-life, then you will likely not have a preference for how your customers migrate from their current solution to a new one. Your primary objective will usually be to maintain a positive image within your customer base and the industry at large. This is often the best case for releasing your software product under an open source license.

Building an Ecosystem

In the previous chapter, I introduced the PalmOS emulator. This is probably one of the earliest examples of a successful and well-executed open source business model. It is also a great example of how a company determined its true value and worked closely with the community at large. It is worth going through the history of how the PalmOS emulator evolved from a community development to something sponsored by a company.

When USRobotics introduced the Pilot family of PDAs to the market, the official development platform was a commercial solution from Metrowerks. Metrowerks specialized in development tools for embedded platforms that ran primarily on the Mac. This was an acceptable solution for commercial developers, but many developers wanted a development solution for the PC platform as well. When writing software for embedded devices such as a PDA, developers will usually want to be able to emulate the device on the development system. This emulation can significantly enhance developer productivity since new software can be rapidly tested, in addition to any changes made through the development cycle. Without an emulator, every developer needs a device, and every change needs to be downloaded to a real, physical device for testing.

While the Metrowerks development suite was a solid and comprehensive development suite, it was far too expensive for the individual developer. The Metrowerks suite was also only available for Mac computers. Since both the Mac and the Pilot shared a microprocessor architecture (the Motorola 68K processor), emulating the device on the Mac was fairly easy. A community of developers gradually started to form around the Pilot (now Palm) PDA. Their goal was to construct a complete, no-cost developer suite that could be used on the PC platform. At the time, open source concepts were not widely known or understood. This community of developers had to reverse-engineer many components of the development value chain. One by one, each of the pieces started to come together. One developer was able to determine the executable format for applications running on the device. Another developer wrote a tool to compile user interface resources. Yet another modified existing open source compilers (GCC) to be able to build and debug applications. In parallel, Greg Hewgill leveraged some emulation work done for other platforms to develop the CoPilot, an emulator for the PC platform. While this is an over-simplification of events, the end result is that the open source community had a comprehensive developer suite for the PC platform that was less sexy than the commercial suite available from Metrowerks, but complete nonetheless.

One of the other key problems Greg needed to solve was the issue of the device ROM. In a PDA, the operating system is contained within read-only memory, or ROM. Greg was doing a pure hardware emulator for the device. But for his emulator to be useful, he needed the software code that was contained within the ROM of the device. With the help of other developers, a tool was written that would extract the entire code from the ROM of an actual device as a collection of small chunks. These chunks were reassembled and loaded into the emulator (note that there are laws today that would likely make this practice illegal and it is not recommended). The platform was now complete. However, since USRobotics had not licensed the ROM software to be passed around this way, every developer had to extract the ROM from the physical device and upload it to his or her emulator. This meant that to develop applications, you still needed to own a PDA.

An interesting dynamic started to occur. The volume of applications available for the Pilot PDA started to increase dramatically. The number of developers writing for the platform started to also increase and a self-feeding ecosystem was well on its way. I can only speculate that USRobotics (followed by 3COM) was having difficulty understanding exactly what was happening. On the one hand, the company was losing control of what was likely perceived as proprietary information about their platform, yet the community of developers was having a very positive effect on the value of the device. As Palm became an independent company, it had a choice to make: Embrace this community, or turn on it and try to regain control. They embraced it. Metrowerks now makes their developer platform available for both the Mac and PC platforms. Commercial developers still use this platform to develop supported applications, but individual hackers have a no-cost platform to develop with. Palm and Metrowerks clearly understood the value of the CoPilot and licensed it from Greg and the other developers involved. In turn, it was renamed the PalmOS emulator (POSE) and licensed under the GPL. POSE is shipped with the PC version of Metrowerks development tools, as well as being available for download by Palm Computing for use by any developer using open source development tools.

Palm Computing has decided that the POSE is a valuable tool required for a complete development suite. However, value is not derived from delivering this tool to their customers; value is derived in delivering a portable computing platform with the broadest possible set of applications. The platform is more valuable with the larger volume of applications available. The emulator is simply an enabler to that end goal.

Palm Computing now works in partnership with the community to continue development of the POSE. Palm assigns internal developers as maintainers of the platform, but the development community continues to provide enhancements and fix defects. In this way, Palm guides ongoing development of the POSE to make sure it stays in step with the evolution of the hardware. It can keep its costs down, and promote a valuable ecosystem by sharing the development of the emulator with the community at large. Palm now makes ROM images available for every new hardware device and new versions of the operating system available for download. It has even extended this to include debug versions of the ROM images to make developers more productive.

This is an example of a business model that demonstrates one of the best ways that open source benefits everyone by allowing a focus on the core value being delivered to the customer, lowering development costs, and accelerating time-to-market:

- Palm Computing correctly determined the value they deliver to their customers: a connected, portable device with a large number of applications.
- The community provided Palm with a valuable ecosystem that promoted its product and made it even more valuable.
- The community developed a key component of the value chain that enabled developers on the PC platform to develop successfully for the product.
- Palm continues to share development of the POSE with the community at large. This active involvement guides the emulator where Palm needs it to go, while leveraging the development know-how of the community.
- Releasing ROM images is a form of releasing documentation that the community needs to be successful. Palm Computing also releases other documentation to help developers be successful.

No one at USRobotics, or 3COM, or now Palm Computing, could have predicted this sequence of events. The opportunity for you is to learn from those who blazed this trail and plan for this type of productive collaboration with the open source community.

Summary

Any of these business models can succeed or fail based on execution alone. Understanding a business model is not a replacement for a comprehensive business analysis. You must still understand your addressable market and customer needs. All of the other elements of building a profitable business are still required. Open source is simply another element that can open opportunities to either build a new business or enhance an existing business.

Now that you have an understanding of the business models available to you, you must understand how to integrate open source within your company. The next chapter will give you the processes and tools that you need to make decisions about using or releasing open source software.

Integrating Open Source into Your Business

*T*he last three chapters went through the details of explaining how open source development works, the economic effects on the software industry, and a variety of business model options to build profitable software businesses within an open source context. Assuming that you believe you can leverage this new software business paradigm, you now need to consider fundamental business process changes. This chapter and the next will outline a set of operational processes to enable you to make sensible decisions when integrating open source software with the various elements of your business. The goals for this chapter are to:

- Detail the valid reasons to make software open source
- Provide a process checklist for moving proprietary software to an open source license
- Learn the issues for incorporating open source into your business
- Understand areas to avoid when working with open source
- Understand the legal issues to consider when integrating with open source

This chapter applies to both IT managers and companies producing commercial software. IT managers will be more likely to bring open source software in-house as a way to reduce costs, and therefore the parts of this chapter dealing with "inbound open source" will be of most interest. Both inbound and outbound (moving proprietary software to an open source license) open source will likely be of interest to commercial software vendors.

Outbound Open Source

Driving an outbound open source initiative refers to taking software currently sold under a proprietary license and moving it to an open source license. To do this successfully, there are a number of steps, as shown in Figure 12–1, to consider to ensure that the project will be successful.

As you can see from Figure 12–1, releasing software to the open source community is not a simple process of throwing code "over the wall." There is some serious planning and detailed thought processes that must take place. Of course, every project is different and some will be more complex than others. In some cases, going through the entire process will take very little time, but the key is making sure you have at least thought through all the elements and you do not get careless. It does not matter how many times a commercial pilot has landed an airplane; he or she will still follow the checklist every time.

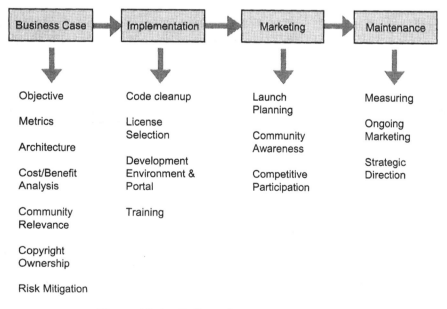

Figure 12–1   Outbound open source process.

Business Case

The first step is to walk through a detailed business case to understand if it even makes sense to proceed with an open source project. Figure 12–1 shows the key elements of the business case. Since following this process will likely be new to you, it is worth going through each element in detail.

Objective

Before engaging in any implementation work, you should make sure that you have sensible objectives for the open source project and that everyone involved is clear about those objectives. Here are some examples, many of them related to the business model discussion of the previous chapter:

- **Devalue a competitive product**—If you have a competitor that has a solution that you do not offer, or a solution that is significantly better than yours, this can be a good reason to proceed. The implication is that your objective is to accelerate the devaluation of your competitors' product and remove that competitors' revenue and profit stream. You must recognize that if you choose to do this, you are affecting the entire market segment for this solution, including yourself.
- **Pervasiveness**—If you have a core infrastructure technology that is an enabler to other products and solutions in your portfolio, then you may want to consider using open source as a method to make your technology pervasive, or adopted as a standard.
- **Cost reduction**—There are times when working collaboratively with the community can reduce the costs of developing a solution. In these instances, you will likely be providing a complex solution to your customers and using open source in certain parts of the stack will allow you to deliver a bigger solution faster and at a lower cost.
- **Hardware**—As I mentioned in the hardware business model discussion, enabling hardware sales is a great reason to work with the open source community.
- **Services and support**—If your primary business model is tied to service delivery, then providing an open source solution can make sense.

- **Exit plan**—If you are exiting a particular business category, open source can be an effective way to accelerate the process and refocus valuable resources.
- **Partner play**—Open source has the effect of encouraging collaboration. You can use open source as a way to work with partners and competitors on very large projects.
- **Documenting prior art**—There may be times when your company has developed technology that is not strategic and does not want to incur the costs of applying for a patent. Releasing software under an open source license is an effective way to document prior art.

Similarly, there are a host of reasons why using open source does not yield a business benefit. Here is a list of the most common reasons for which using open source is generally not a good idea:

- **Control point**—If your product is a competitive control point, or generates a significant barrier to entry for your competitors, then you should not consider open source for a product.
- **Product obsolescence**—End-of-life may not be the same as an obsolete product. If a product is no longer useful in your eyes and those of your customers, then terminate the product. Attempting to keep the product alive through open source is generally not a very good reason to use open source.
- **Negative cost/benefit**—If you do the financial analysis of what it will take to move to an open source license, you should be able to quantify a larger return, or do not execute.
- **Resource defocus**—Usually when moving a product to the open source community, you will still need to apply internal resources. If the application and cost of those resources significantly defocuses the organization, then it may not be a good idea to move ahead.
- **IP risk**—Your attorneys need to work with you to understand who owns the IP in a product. If the legal IP risks are too great, or are difficult to quantify, then you should not proceed with the project.
- **Competing with the community**—Competing with an existing open source project is generally not a good idea and will generate ill will with the community. If a project similar to yours already exists, you should attempt to join and enhance the project rather than compete with it. There are times when competing projects with different goals can make sense. Take time to consider your options carefully in this scenario and seek guidance from the community.

- **It's cool!**—Many engineers will believe that because they have developed very good and very cool technology that it should be open sourced. The view is that positive press can be garnered. In most cases, the short-term positive press will be offset by long-term costs and negative press when the project does not measure up to initial expectations.

When your team has determined the key goals for the project, you can move to the next stage of building the business case.

Metrics

Once you understand the objectives for your project, you should set up a set of metrics. These metrics will be important when you build your risk mitigation plan, and when you attempt to measure if your project was successful. Some of the key metrics to monitor (based on your objectives) include:

- Your competitor reducing the price of a competitive product
- The number of developers actively contributing to your project
- The actual number of contributions
- The number of users downloading and using the project
- Ecosystem components building around your project
- Lowered development costs with better time-to-market compared to the status quo

The metrics depend on the specifics of the project, but it is important that you understand how to define success and over what time period you expect to see success.

Architecture

The architecture phase involves technical resources early in the decision lifecycle. A technology specialist needs to assess the architecture of the proposed open source project. The determinations that the technical team needs to make are:

- Do we have a clear separation of modules in the software?
- Can the software be partitioned effectively between proprietary and open source components?
- If the goal of the open source project is to enable proprietary projects, are the interfaces in place to enable the proprietary components to stay that way?

- Can the software be isolated and extracted from existing corporate configuration management systems?
- Do you own all of the IP of the software being proposed for open source? If not, do you have a license to release it under an open source license, or can you replace the affected component?
- Are there licensed patents covering the code being released? Even if you have a patent cross-license with another vendor, you may not have the rights to further license that patent under an open source license.

Every project will be different and every software architecture unique. If you have established a clear objective for the project, then it will guide the technical team to make the right assessment to prepare the software product for release.

Cost/Benefit Analysis

Many people believe that the process of moving software to an open source license only requires a simple packaging exercise and making the product available for download. However, it can be far more expensive to open source products than this simple view of the world. Each financial analysis must take into consideration the goals and dynamics of the specific project. There are some common elements that should be considered as part of the cost analysis:

- Maintaining a new software repository.
- Sanitizing the existing code base and removing any inappropriate components or comments.
- Marketing programs to announce the availability of the project and building a community.
- Performing ongoing maintenance of the software (assuming you choose to remain the maintainer of the software).
- Making documentation available. Documentation would include architecture, design, and end-user documentation.
- Hosting software portals that allow a community to work together and participate in the project. You can host this yourself or use the services of third parties.
- Incurring training costs depending on the complexity of the software project being released.
- Accumulating download costs. If you are releasing a popular software solution, you may need to set up servers to handle increased download traffic. Whether you do this yourself or contract it to a third party, the costs can be significant.

You should expect these costs to be balanced with a return. That return should be directly tied to the goals of the project, but would take the form of one or more of the following:

- Reduced internal development costs
- Reduced support costs
- Increased visibility in the marketplace
- Greater revenue of companion products (hardware and software)
- An acceptable degree of damage to your competitor(s)

This cost/benefit analysis will give you the information you need to ensure that you are making a decision grounded in fundamental business value.

Community Relevance

This is an important but often overlooked component of the decision process. While many open source advocates believe that all software should be made available publicly, you just saw that there is a list of very real costs to consider. It only makes sense to proceed with an open source project if you can recover those costs in tangible and intangible ways. There are times when releasing your software to the community will not generate any excitement. No one will care, and no one will participate in the development of your project.

It is critical to determine ahead of time if you will have a community develop around your project. If you are adding functionality to an existing project area, you will generally be able to contact the leaders of the sub-community ahead of time and get a clear indication of the willingness to participate in your development project.

In the case where you are attempting to build a community from existing customers, you should poll a significant number of your customers to get a feel for their desire and willingness to invest resources in participating in a development community.

Finally, if your goal is to create a brand new community for a new technology area, you should plan very comprehensive marketing programs to promote the project and you should not underestimate the costs of running such a project. You will also need to seek out and even provide incentives to prospective developers in your new community.

Copyright Ownership

Although I mentioned the issue of copyright ownership earlier, it is worth noting that this needs to be a conscious part of the decision-making process. Not only must you consider the existing ownership of the code base, but you must also decide if you wish to obtain the copyright for any contributions from the community.

Part of this decision process will be based on the business model you have selected. If you recall from the previous chapter, you can release your software under two distinct licenses: one open source and the other proprietary. If you have chosen a dual-license business model, then you will need to ensure that you have processes established to accept contributions from those who are willing to reassign the copyright back to you, or that you have a license that permits you to sub-license.

Risk Mitigation

Obviously you have every intention that your project will go well. However, you should consider the negative sides of execution. Admitting that things may go wrong and preparing for them makes good business sense. Elements you should consider as part of your risk mitigation plan include:

- What if no community forms around your project? How long will you wait for the community to gain its footing? If a community is not taking hold, what additional marketing programs are you willing to pay for to make it successful? What are your decision criteria to terminate the project?
- What if the anticipated costs of the project exceed expectations? Do you have planned contingencies for cost overruns?
- What if the IP of the project is contested? Do you have proper documentation available for any license agreements?
- What if a competing project forms? Do you understand the conditions you should work with to avoid a competing project?
- What if a community creates an alternate project with a different strategic direction based on your project? What will be your public reaction? Do you care?
- What if the downloads far exceed your expectations and users cannot get to the software? What processes have you developed to handle unexpected loads?

Always take the time to consider what may go wrong. Do not take a pessimistic view of the project; just build smart business contingencies.

Implementation

After going through the business case development process, you should have enough information to make a go/no-go decision. If you get to the implementation phase, then you have made the decision to proceed with your project and it is now time to make the plan operational.

Code Cleanup

Implementation begins with code cleanup to ensure you have a source base that you can release to the public. The elements of code cleanup include:

- **Making sure what you are releasing can be built with minimal instructions and is fully functional**—The community will react negatively to nonfunctional software. This does not mean defect-free, but it should be stable enough that others can understand how the product works.
- **Structuring and commenting the code**—This can be a complex task if you are extracting the code from a larger project. Consider that a group of outsiders needs to understand how the code works. The easier you make it for them to understand, the more likely it is you will receive contributions.
- **Sanitizing the code**—You need to ensure that any comments, coding conventions, and other parts of the project do not contain proprietary information. This is usually in the form of employee names, product code names, and future product intent. You may also need to clean out derogatory comments that may have been included by some of your engineers.
- **Validate the IP status of the code**—You need to make sure that the code you are releasing was either written entirely by you and your employees or that you have valid licenses to distribute the code. If your contractors contributed to your code, did they assign their copyright to you in their contract or grant you sufficient license rights so that you can include it with your code? Verify also that you have patent rights to use, sell, and offer for sale the code embodying the patents. Consult an experienced IP attorney for this step.

You also need to include detailed build instructions and document any other dependencies such as external libraries and their versions. Releasing good-quality code is a big part of building a vibrant community. You and your engineers need to take this step very seriously.

License Selection

You need to undertake this step with the help of your legal council. Chapter 3 explained that there are over 30 licenses currently approved by the OSI. If at all possible, you should select one of the licenses currently available. The first step is deciding if you want a license with a reciprocity provision (a license that forces contributions to be returned to the community). If your goal is to create a community with an incentive to innovate and grow your project, then you should look at such reciprocal licenses, the most common being the GPL and LGPL. However, if you want to allow others to take your software and create other proprietary solutions, then a BSD or MIT license may be the most appropriate. Of course, as I already mentioned, you may choose to dual-license your solution.

Whatever license you select, you should attempt to develop a consistent strategy for all the open source projects you may eventually release to the community. A consistent strategy does not imply the same license for all projects, but rather a coherent license selection for similar project types. This way, the outside world will have a consistent set of expectations from your company. This would become part of an overall corporate open source strategy.

Development Environment

You need to select the development environment, tools, and processes you will use to work with your community. This can be as simple as packaging your software solution, making it available for download, and never looking at it again. Obviously, this is not the best way to create a collaborative community. Most will use the tools commonly accepted by the majority of open source projects and discussed in previous chapters. It is possible to build more informal sharing processes with simple tools such as email. Depending on the project, you may want to create discussion groups to encourage communication among all those in your community.

You also need to know how you plan to host your project. You may choose to use internal company servers or the services of third parties to host your project. Whatever route you choose, your hosting selection should be closely tied to your marketing programs to drive the maximum traffic to your project.

Training

Training is not usually considered part of the process of releasing open source software, but it should be. Considering training should also be part of your marketing program. Most developers will not be able to attend training classes or be able to travel to any location. You should consider formal training only if you are building a community built on your customer base and the training is part of an overall solution program.

Of course, you can consider electronic training methods as simple as good documentation and as complex as comprehensive Web seminars.

Marketing

For those who believe that taking software to an open source license is a simple process of packaging the code and making it available for download, the idea of a comprehensive marketing program will seem somewhat foreign. But, successful projects will have good, sustained marketing programs. The key elements of your marketing program will include some or all of the elements that follow.

Launch Planning

Planning the launch of your project is a critical component that will involve getting key members on-board from the community. If you have the ability to quote well-known members in a press release, that will help your launch activity. If you have well-known industry partners involved in the project, you should attempt to have them join your launch. Projects tied to specific industries should attempt to synchronize their launches with well-publicized industry events.

Community Awareness

You need to build an awareness that will encourage developers to come and participate in your development project. You need to focus your awareness campaign on the topical area of interest. The term "community" is a generic term that refers to any group of developers. Clearly, if you are building a human resources application, you do not want to target kernel hackers.

Competitive Participation

Working with your competitors will usually be the result of recognizing that no one organization can afford the complete development cost of the project when all will share in the results. For some industries, working with competitors is a fact of life and will be par for the course.

In other industries, joining in a project with your competitors will seem strange at first. But, when you internalize that the open nature of the project ensures that everyone is participating equally, you will get more and more comfortable with the notion. Consult your attorney so that you can avoid antitrust behavior; the law limits the kinds of cooperation you can have with your competitors.

Maintenance

The maintenance phase begins when the project is public, you have executed your marketing plan, and if all goes well, a community begins to form around your project. This phase needs to be actively managed to ensure that your success goals are being met and that the project continues to go in the direction you envisioned. For most projects, you will also need to keep up the marketing and awareness campaign.

Measuring

In the business planning phase you should have defined some success metrics, including items such as the number of contributors and contributions, downloads or requests for the software, etc. You should collect each metric on a predetermined timeline and initiate actions based on the results of the metrics. For example, if the number of contributors is not living up to expectations, you might turn up the heat on your marketing campaign, or gather intelligence from early contributors that might help build a plan for increasing the contributions. Whatever metrics you develop, measure the results and react when the measures are either above or below expectations.

Ongoing Marketing

You should avoid a scenario where you launch your project but do not have the plan and budget to keep the awareness going. Industry events occur frequently and your project can often be connected to any one of those events. For example, if your project is a software program targeted at mobile devices and the industry releases new products or standards related to mobility, you might be able to latch on to an event to raise the visibility of your project. This is an ongoing effort and it needs to be someone's job to monitor the industry and take every opportunity to connect your project to these events.

There is also always a new stream of developers joining the industry. What was common knowledge a year ago is new information for many entrants to your industry. Constant updates, refreshes, and education are the keys to ensuring that your community stays fresh and vibrant.

Strategic Direction

One of the most wonderful things about open source (which will make many managers uncomfortable) is that the community will often take your project in directions you might not have predicted. Portions of your software may be used in other, unrelated areas, in ways you could not have anticipated. In most cases, you should view these as positive events. They are signs of a community that is alive, growing, and sustaining itself. But, you must also take care to ensure that the direction of the project is consistent with the objectives you established during the business planning phase.

A very interesting dynamic can occur here and it needs to be monitored closely. It is possible that the community will want to take your project in a different direction than you had anticipated; this new direction may be better than your original plan. This will require you to have a very open mind and consider the new options being presented to you. However, it is your role to establish leadership and communicate the strategic vision of the project. You just need to make sure you don't get so myopic that you ignore great opportunities that are dropped in your lap. An attitude of "not invented here (NIH)" is not useful.

Inbound Open Source

The process of taking existing open source software and integrating it as part of a product, or used within an internal IT project, is known as "inbound open source." The rules and processes associated with doing this are radically different than when you do outbound open source and the business processes you establish need to be even more rigorous in nature. Here is a list of valid business reasons to look at bringing open source software within your organization:

- **Standards**—If there is an open source implementation of a key industry standard that is important to your business, then building your products on this standard may be good thing. You will not have to re-implement your own version of the standard.
- **Existing technology**—If the community has already developed a technology that has become pervasive, then using that technology will often be the most effective way to drive your product forward.

- **Resources**—If the licenses and structure of the open source technology (discussed next) are such that you can effectively use the technology as a foundation for your product, then open source can be a very effective way to focus available resources on higher value-added capabilities that you can use to generate more revenue.
- **No reciprocity risk**—The GPL, LGPL, and a few other open source licenses contain reciprocity provisions that require you to return any changes or enhancements to the community. It is therefore important that you evaluate the risk of mixing GPL code, for example, with a proprietary code that you will subsequently be distributing.

Similarly, there are few cases where bringing open source software into your organization or integrating it into an internal project should be avoided:

- **Strategic direction**—Although the open source project may meet your immediate needs, its future direction may be inconsistent with your business goals. You should endeavor to work with the project maintainer to understand where he or she would like to drive the project. If you ignore the stated intent of the project, you could find yourself supporting the project on your own.
- **Technical assessment**—If your key technical leads on the project do not agree with the use of open source software as part of the overall architecture, then a deeper analysis is required at a minimum. You may need to balance valid architectural concerns with a cultural aversion to trying something new. Make sure that your technical team is making the best assessment for the business and that you push for options that would allow the use of the open source project.
- **Release control**—As you now well understand, the community will release software when the maintainer determines the time is right. If you need absolute control over time-to-market and this component has upcoming features that are critical to your release, you may not be able to afford the dependency. Of course, the way in which you should deal with this condition is to engage with the community and make contributions that will meet the needs of your project.

Figure 12–2 is a simplified view of a process you can follow to ensure that inbound open source is done with the correct level of business controls.

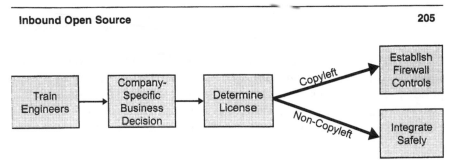

Figure 12–2   Inbound open source process.

This figure demonstrates that the first step you must follow is to make sure you have a well-trained set of engineers.

Training the Engineers

It is too easy for an engineer to go to the Internet, find useful code, and integrate it into your source base. The problem is that unless you educate your engineering talent, they may integrate code, such as GPL-licensed code, into your proprietary software, such that it affects the proprietary status of your software. Those who try to pitch doom-like scenarios will assert that the end result is that your entire code base must immediately be made available under the same reciprocal license. No court has ever required such a drastic result. The more likely scenario is that the offending GPL or other open source code must be removed from your source base as soon as it is discovered. However, this can still be an expensive proposition, which is why training is critical.

A much greater concern than exposing your IP in an uncontrolled way is the need to recall a product you have delivered to your customers. Therefore, it is critical that your engineers are well-trained on the implications of extracting code from unknown sources and clearly understand the implications to your business.

Company-Specific Decisions

As you develop more competence with open source, your company should develop policies that cover the appropriate use and methods for integration with open source. Obviously, this book is about giving you enough information to recognize the tremendous benefits that can come with using open source software. However, even if you decide to implement a policy that completely disallows open source within your organization, you cannot ignore the fact that it is incredibly easy for engineers to grab code from Internet sources. Therefore your policy must be explicit and communicated to all of your engineers.

Your company needs to make its own decisions to allow the integration of open source. Your policy needs to cover:

- What project classes should consider using open source software
- What licenses or class of licenses you will allow
- Employee behavior when working with company resources and accessing software under an open source license
- How the software is managed within the organization
- Support processes for released software that includes open source

The next chapter will cover more detailed employee issues related to open source software that will help you make the right decisions for your employees and your business.

Determining the License

As you now understand, there is a class of license that incorporates a reciprocity provision which dictates that contributions be returned to the community. The GPL and LGPL are the most common. If this is the type of license for the code you will integrate, then you need to establish the proper engineering controls to ensure that open source code is not mixed with proprietary code unless that is your specific intent.

If the license does not contain a reciprocity provision, for example a BSD or MIT, then you can safely integrate the code within your project. You should still consider working proactively with the community, developing the code so that you can share the support burden should anything go wrong.

Firewall

If your company is maintaining proprietary software and open source software, it is critical that you have processes established to maintain a firewall between the two environments. The best way to ensure this happens is to maintain two different software configuration management systems, or to only use the public open source repository for the open source code. You should also consider the assignments of your engineers. If you have a single engineer working on both proprietary code and open source code, then that engineer needs to be very well-trained to ensure that he or she does not inappropriately move open source code to the proprietary code base unless the open source license permits that combination. Even in cases where engineering teams are kept separate, a team should still be trained to avoid situations where it shares code and may lose track of the license on the code.

IT Development

If you are doing internal software development and never plan to release software to the public, then you can extract open source code, use it, and not worry about how it is integrated into your environment. All open source licenses permit that use without affecting your proprietary software; only subsequent redistribution would be constrained. If you choose to do this, you should consider the potential negative consequences you will have to deal with:

- If you take the code and never return contributions, then you are on your own from that point on. *You* need to support the software thereafter.
- Should the company ever decide to commercialize your internal project, you could have significant dependencies on open source components that have not been well-architected to allow for a clean separation from the software you developed internally.

The best approach is always to work collaboratively with the community, and properly architect clean separations between proprietary and open source software.

Indemnification

If you are delivering commercial software and typically integrate software from a third party, your contract with that third party will often contain indemnification provisions. One purpose of an indemnity provision is to ensure that if the software you are licensing uses another person's IP without permission, you are not the one held liable. Most open source licenses do not provide that form of indemnification provision. The nature of most open source software is that it incorporates elements from many different sources, and many of those sources may not be traceable.

Even if a major corporation "sells" open source software as part of a larger commercial offering, it may not be possible for that company to indemnify you against any IP claims.

The industry is gradually getting more aware of this notion of no indemnification. For example, in many cases, you cannot be held liable for software that can be downloaded freely from the Internet.

Summary

This chapter gave you the foundation to make solid business decisions when integrating open source within your business. You should now have an understanding of what it means to take your software and release it to the community, as well as take open source code and integrate it within your company. You should have nearly all the framework components you need to develop a policy specific to your company that covers open source usage.

The final elements we need to cover are related to human resources issues. Some of the human resources components will help complete your company's open source policy and other elements will ensure that you hire the right team and work well with the community.

Human Resources—
Getting Top Talent

Many companies have employment policies that stipulate that the company owns anything its employees develop. What happens when an employee works on an open source project? How is it possible for your employee to give away their developments while fulfilling the requirements of his or her employment agreement? Open source fundamentally changes how you view human resources and organizational development. In this chapter, we will examine the details of how the hiring process needs to change, the new qualifications that you need to look for, and some of the IP provisions normally associated with the hiring process. We will also examine the notion of the community as an extension of the organization and managing the organizational firewalls. Your goals for this chapter are to understand how to:

- Evolve your recruiting and hiring processes
- Manage the IP ownership among employee, company, and community
- Manage community leaders in your company

Hiring and working with the community of developers is a different process, but it allows you to know and understand who you are hiring and what skills they have very early in that process.

Employment Contracts

When you hire engineering talent that has been working within the Linux community and hold very strong beliefs about open source and free software, you will likely encounter a new request from these employees during the hiring phase. Such a prospective employee will be excited about coming to work with a company that is involved in open source projects. However, that person may also have very clear expectations that the only projects they will ever work on are open source projects. Your company needs to develop a clear set of policies governing existing and new employee hires. Your new policies should consider the following elements:

- **Projects**—Can a new or existing employee limit his or her contributions to open source projects? For large companies that know they will have long, sustained engagements with the community, this may be fine. However, if you expect employees to participate in proprietary projects, your policy needs to be clear.

- **Copyright ownership**—As you have learned throughout this book, even open source contributions involve copyright ownership. Your policy should dictate who is expected to own the copyright for contributions by your engineers. Is it owned by the company, the employee, or both? In most cases, the company should retain the copyright ownership (or acceptable license) to be able to implement dual-licensing should the need arise. There may be cases such as Apache and SAMBA when it will not be possible for your company to retain the copyright on contributions. These projects have policies that prevent you from retaining copyright ownership.

- **Personal vs. company time**—Many engineers will work on open source projects in their spare time. In some cases, the line between company-related work and employee hobby will be clear; in others it will not. In yet other cases, what an employee starts as a hobby project may evolve into a company-relevant project. You need to clearly define when and how your engineers can participate in open source projects on their personal time, and define the disclosure rules for your employees. Local employment laws may limit restrictions on your employees.

- **Competition**—Your human resources policy will likely restrict your employees' abilities to work with competitors. One of the fundamental benefits of open source is that sometimes it is best to share the developments and costs with your competitors (within the limits of antitrust law). In these cases, your engineers may be actively involved with your competitors in development projects.

If your set of policies and guidelines covers these elements, you should be able to work on open source projects and take advantage of the talent that is available.

Participation Policies

Make it clear to your employees what the business objectives are. Some engineers will need to be reminded that your company is in the business of making a profit. Even if they work on a project that will not generate direct revenue, they should understand where the business intends to make money (e.g., support, services, hardware, etc.). A clear communication of your business model will help your engineers ensure that they participate in the most effective way possible with the community, while applying the right degree of judgment when decisions need to be made on where the lines between open source and proprietary software need to be drawn.

You also need to define your behavior with the community. What are the acceptable licenses that a project must have for employees to participate? If you work on Linux kernel projects, what will be your policy on proprietary and open source kernel modules? In short, use the elements of this chapter, and the other elements you have learned from the rest of this book, to develop a comprehensive open source policy and strategy that define for your employees and the community what your expectations are for a respectable code of conduct and how you intend to partner with the community.

Hiring the Right Person

During the hiring process, you are trying to assess if an individual is a fit as a new employee within the organization. There are now an additional set of criteria you need to look for in a prospective candidate. This list does not replace your standard hiring processes. You should consider these additional criteria to evaluate during the hiring process.

Technology

Each technology (Linux kernel, file system, Web server, device drivers, networking stacks, etc.) area will have a sub-community. Although your prospective candidate may not be well-known in the larger community, a prospective employee may be one of the best-known developers for the area you are looking for. Therefore, do not focus so much on overall notoriety in the Linux and open source community, but look for respect within the focused sub-communities you care about. Contact members of that sub-community and get to know who the players are.

Community Home

Each project has a maintainer. The maintainer is responsible for accepting or rejecting contributions to the source base and deciding when a release is appropriate. New communities can spawn from disagreements between a maintainer and a contributor, an event referred to as "forking" (although this is rare). This can be the healthiest part of the open source process. However, there are cases when competing projects are not desirable (such as the Linux kernel). The better maintainers will have a proven track record of resolving conflict and focusing all the development energy for a given technology area on a single project. It is possible for you to hire the maintainer for a given project. You will then need to balance your needs for that individual carrying out their company duties and their responsibilities to their community. Is your company able to deal with a situation where the maintainer/employee makes a decision that is right for the open source community but disadvantageous for the company? *Do not assume that because you hire the maintainer, you control the project! Recall that Linus is the maintainer of the Linux kernel, not his current employer, Transmeta.*

Maintainer or Contributor

As you now understand very well, most open source projects are characterized by having a maintainer and a community of contributors. You need to have a clear understanding of the role you are trying to fill. You will only need so many chiefs, and having a strong pool of contributors is critical to your success. Finding individuals who have experience in making contributions in many different technology areas will be a big plus. They will have a clear understanding of how different communities operate, and they will have been exposed to a number of different maintainer styles. It is a good idea to contact the maintainer of any project a contributor has been involved in to gauge the quality and value of those contributions.

If you decide that you need to fill a leadership role, look for someone who has previous experience maintaining an open source project. As a maintainer, test some of the following leadership characteristics:

- Does he/she recognize and give credit to key contributors?
- How does he/she resolve conflicts between contributors?
- Has he/she seen competing projects created as a result of not resolving conflict? Was it the right outcome?
- Has he/she been able to attract key contributors to his/her project?
- Has he/she developed release processes?
- What process does he/she use to determine that a project is ready for release?
- Can he/she give examples of contributions that were better than his/her own implementations?

Maintainers are a special breed of individuals who combine technical skills with the ability to interact well with other developers and guide the development of a project.

Community Visibility and Respect

The ability to drive an agenda within the community is dependent on the degree of active involvement and real contributions to the project. Recall that control is with the maintainer. The maintainer of the project will be influenced by familiarity with the individual(s) making contributions, plus the quality of those contributions. Does the prospective candidate have positive visibility and respect within the community? To determine the level of respect and visibility, look at the online interactions your candidate has with the community (e.g., mailing lists, archives, etc.).

Online Interactions

Once you understand the community(ies) that your candidate is involved in, and you believe you have a strong fit with your specific needs, spend time understanding how the individual interacts with others online. Online interactions will be the primary vehicle for communication with others. It is vital that the candidate is able to wield influence with others in disparate time zones and cultures. Here are some things to look for:

- Ask for, or go to, email archives and examine the interactions. Look for the interaction style of your candidate. Does it fit with your company's culture, and does it appear effective in getting contributions accepted?
- Discover what pseudonyms your candidate uses online. Look at the archives at SlashDot (see the reference section at the back of this book) and other online locales. Does your candidate hide behind secret pseudonyms to trash other individuals? Is there passion without condemnation?
- Does your candidate initiate discussion on useful, compelling topics? Or, does your candidate only respond to others? Are the responses constructive?

Attempt to determine the respect your candidate has by looking at how many seek out his/her advice. Also examine how readily contributions are accepted by other maintainers. Someone who has developed respect within a community will be able to get his/her contributions accepted with virtually no debate.

Contributions

Request a detailed list of actual contributions to a variety of open source projects. When evaluating candidates from competing companies, it is not possible to request actual contributions to proprietary products. The beauty of open source is that everything is open and public. You have the ability to measure the quantity, quality, and technical capability of your candidate before ever hiring. Your managers and other employees are a good source to use to analyze historical contributions and give you the feedback you need.

Also look for the style of contributions. Does the candidate make tactical contributions to solve specific problems and patch specific issues, or does he/she get involved in architectural and design discussions? The style of contributions should fit the needs of the position you are trying to fill, as well as build your bench strength for leaders of the future. For example, if you are trying to fill a support position, someone who has the ability to find problems and fix them without negatively affecting the overall system can be very valuable. However, if you need to find someone who will be a maintainer and guide architectural direction, you need to look for someone who has a track record of identifying and acknowledging stellar work from others.

Geography

Anyone with experience in working with the open source community will be capable of working and interacting with people across geographies, time zones, and cultures. The challenge for the hiring manager will be to develop a geography strategy for talent acquisition, as well as where the talent resides after hiring.

It can be a great benefit to your company to be able to hire talent from anywhere in the world and have them join your team. However, this will need to be balanced with the obvious benefits of having a co-located team that can work closely together. From my experience, one of the best strategies is to ensure that you have a strong critical mass in one location for a given project. Avoid splitting projects across geographic boundaries. Then you can add specialized, high-caliber talent in remote geographies that supports and enhances a local team. The other benefit to this is that when your team works with outside community members, it manages the relationship to remote company members virtually the same way as community members.

If you are contributing to an open source project that is critical to your company, consider funding a face-to-face meeting on a periodic basis for the key members of this community. This is often called a "hackfest." If you can plan this around an industry event related to the business, then you can bring all the developers together to learn about the industry, get to know each other, and get some serious development accomplished. Plan to pay for airfare, hotel, meals, and all the usual expenses that a regular employee would have. You will generally find that community participants are frugal and more interested in getting development done than wasting your money. Your goal should be to get through a critical development crunch by supplying all the equipment the team needs. This way, the co-location and resultant collaboration will yield significant results.

Count the Hops

A community is largely driven by influence. The ultimate point of influence is the maintainer of a project. For large projects, there will be an informal hierarchy of trust between the maintainer and key contributors. Obviously, it is not realistic to always expect to be able to hire the maintainer of a project. In the hiring process, discover and understand this hierarchy and then count the number of developers between your prospective hire and the final control point, the maintainer. This is known as "counting the hops," like one does in network traffic routing. The less hops, the closer the candidate is to the maintainer.

Structuring the Teams

Structuring your teams will largely depend on the role your company takes in an open source project. As you learned from the corporate bazaar concept, it is possible for you to structure a very large open source project and manage the team. More often, you will be working on much smaller projects; in many cases, you will be one of many contributors to an open source project.

Because of the reciprocity issues outlined in the previous chapter, you should make every effort to keep developers contributing to external projects dedicated to open source projects.

The special case of gated communities will also come into play when structuring your development teams. You may find yourself with a combination of proprietary projects, open source projects, and projects within gated communities. It will be up to you to ensure that you have defined detailed processes to ensure that IP ownership and developer assignments are clearly defined for each of the boundaries.

Hiring Visible Leaders

At this late point in the book, I will share a specific and personal experience from within the HP context. By many peoples' measure, I took a significant risk when I hired a visible and vocal open source community leader, Bruce Perens. Bruce's first priority continues to be to represent the community at large and to advance the open source movement. He works with a number of internal HP product teams to offer advice and education related to working with the open source community. Bruce also represents HP with a number of our customers. On some rare occasions, Bruce's opinions are different than those of the company's. Bruce and I have worked on a set of rules to guide these conditions:

- Bruce cannot make personal attacks on HP and its executives.
- Bruce cannot share proprietary product information until it is publicly released.
- Bruce must clearly identify when he speaks his own opinion representing the community rather than that of HP's.

It was also my job to work with the industry, the press, analysts, customers, partners, and competitors to ensure that they clearly understood Bruce's role within HP. In my estimation, while Bruce's dual role continues to cause a small degree of discomfort with some management teams within HP, it has been very positive to our Linux and open source business. Most people in the industry have adapted very well to the dual role that community leaders need to have. Both Bruce and HP have been able to maintain a high degree of credibility and integrity.

Open source leaders must represent their community first and company second. It will be difficult for you to accept this concept at first, but if you establish clear boundaries for communication, it can be successful. Make sure your employees understand that this individual has a unique role and that you are not redefining the behavior code for the company. Make sure you develop a solid, trusting relationship between your company and any visible leader you might hire.

Summary

Structuring, building, and managing teams that combine open source and non-open source projects is a different way to manage engineering teams. Culturally, your engineers will struggle between their loyalty to the community and their loyalty to the company. You need to be aware of this cross-loyalty challenge that many of your developers will have and get accustomed to managing it, and not feel threatened by it. This chapter gave you the new items you need to consider as part of the hiring and management process, and the elements you should consider as part of developing company policy.

References
and Resources

This appendix is a compendium of resources for you to use to quickly locate information about topics of interest in the Linux and open source worlds. Remember that the Internet is constantly changing. The links provided here were current at the time of publication, but change is inevitable.

Linux

Linux:
http://www.linux.org/

Linux kernel:
http://www.kernel.org/

Alpha Linux Organization:
http://www.linuxalpha.org/

Linux on ARM:
http://www.armlinux.org/

Linux on PA-RISC:
http://www.parisc-linux.org/

Linux on PowerPC:
http://www.linuxppc.org/
http://www.linuxppc.com/

Linux on SPARC/UltraSPARC:
http://www.ultralinux.org/

Linux Distributions

Caldera:
http://www.caldera.com/

Connectiva:
http://www.connectiva.com/

Debian:
http://www.debian.org/

Red Hat:
http://www.redhat.com/

SuSE:
http://www.suse.com/

TurboLinux:
http://www.turbolinux.com/

Red Flag:
http://www.redflag-linux.com/eindex.html

MontaVista:
http://www.mvista.com/

MandrakeSoft:
http://www.linux-mandrake.com/en

UnitedLinux
http://www.unitedlinux.com/

Licenses

Apache Software License:
http://xml.apache.org/fop/license.html

GNU GPL:
http://www.fsf.org/licenses/gpl.html

GNU LGPL:
http://www.fsf.org/licenses/lgpl.html

GNU Free Documentation License:
http://www.fsf.org/licenses/fdl.html

Microsoft shared source licensing program and details:
http://www.microsoft.com/licensing/sharedsource/default.asp

Netscape Public License (NPL):
http://www.mozilla.org/MPL/NPL-1.0.html

SUN community source license principles:
http://www.sun.com/981208/scsl/principles.html

Newsgroups and Publications

Linux Journal:
http://www.linuxjournal.com/

Linux Magazine:
http://www.linuxmagazine.com/

Linux Today:
http://www.linuxtoday.com/

SlashDot:
http://slashdot.org/

NewsForge:
http://newsforge.com/

Organizations

Embedded Linux Consortium:
http://www.embedded-linux.org/

Free Software Foundation (FSF):
http://www.fsf.org/

Free Standards Group (FSG):
http://www.freestandards.org/

GNOME Foundation:
http://foundation.gnome.org/

KDE League:
http://www.kdeleague.org/

Linux International:
http://www.li.org/

Open Source Development Lab (OSDL):
http://www.osdlab.org/

Open Source Development Network:
http://www.osdn.com/

Open Source Initiative (OSI):
http://www.opensource.org/

Pharmaceutical Research and Manufacturers of America:
http://www.phrma.org/

SourceForge:
http://sourceforge.net/

Savannah:
http://savannah.gnu.org/

Open Source Links

The GNU Project:
http://www.gnu.org/

Open Source Definition (OSD):
http://www.opensource.org/docs/definition.html

Debian Social Contract:
http://www.debian.org/social_contract

Open Source Projects

Apache:
http://www.apache.org/

Beowulf clusters:
http://www.beowulf.org/

Ext2 file system:
http://e2fsprogs.sourceforge.net/ext2.html

GCC compiler and tool chain:
http://gcc.gnu.org/

GNOME desktop:
http://www.gnome.org/

Handheld Linux:
http://www.handhelds.org/

IBM JFS:
http://oss.software.ibm.com/developer/opensource/jsf/

JBOSS application server:
http://www.jboss.org/

KDE desktop:
http://www.kde.org/

Linux documentation project:
http://www.linuxdoc.org/

Mozilla Web browser:
http://www.mozilla.org/

MySQL:
http://www.mysql.org/

Open Office:
http://www.openoffice.org/

PalmOS Emulator:
http://www.palmos.com/dev/tools/emulator/

Perl:
http://www.perl.org/

PostgreSQL database:
http://www.postgresql.org/

Python:
http://www.python.org/

SAMBA:
http://www.samba.org/

TUX Web server:
http://www.redhat.com/products/software/linux/tux

Reiser journaling file system:
http://www.namesys.com/

SGI XFS:
http://oss.sgi.com/projects/xfs

XFree86:
http://www.xfree.org/

Papers and Books

"The Cathedral and the Bazaar":
http://www.tuxedo.org/~esr/writings/cathedral-bazaar/cathedral-bazaar/

O'Reilly Books:
http://www.oreilly.com/

Standards

Free Standards Group (FSG):
http://www.freestandards.org/

Linux Standards Base (LSB):
http://www.linuxbase.org/

Linux internationalization:
http://www.li18nux.org/

Training

CompTIA:
http://www.comptia.org/certification/linuxplus/index.htm

Linux training:
http://www.linuxtraining.com/

Linux Professional Institute (LPI):
http://www.lpi.org/

SAIR Linux:
http://www.linuxcertification.com/

Software Listings and Downloads

FreshMeat:
http://www.freshmeat.net/

Sample Copyright Assignment

This Copyright Assignment applies to certain software that is an original work of authorship (the "Software") owned by _____ (hereinafter "Contributor"). The Software is further described in Attachment 1 hereto.

For good and valuable consideration, the sufficiency of which is hereby acknowledged, _____ (hereinafter "Open Source Project") and Contributor hereby agree as follows:

1. Contributor hereby agrees to assign and does hereby assign to Open Source Project its copyright in the Software, including any accompanying documentation files and supporting files as well as the actual program source code.

2. Open Source Project hereby agrees to grant back and does hereby grant back to Contributor a non-exclusive, royalty-free and non-cancelable license to use the Software as Contributor sees fit, including for the creation of derivative works thereof. This license does not limit Open Source Project's rights and public rights acquired through this Copyright Assignment.

3. Open Source Project has all the rights of a copyright owner in the assigned copyrights, subject only to the grant back license to Contributor defined in paragraph 2, including the right to enforce the copyrights in aid of the development of open source software, the right to license and distribute the Software, the right to create derivative works based on the Software, and the

right to use, license and distribute said derivative works with the Software or as stand-alone modules.

4. Contributor will report, upon request of Open Source Project and to the extent actually known to Contributor, any outstanding rights or claims of rights of any person that might be adverse to the rights of Contributor or Open Source Project in the Software.

5. The parties shall execute such documents and undertake such acts as may be requested by the other to implement the letter and spirit of this Copyright Assignment and any conveyance stated herein, subject to a limitation of reasonableness of such request with attention to cost and time burdens imposed thereby. The undertakings in this paragraph are without prejudice to the conveyances made through this Copyright Assignment. The intention of Open Source Project and Contributor is that this assignment document will be supplemented rarely, if at all, by other documents.

6. Contributor hereby agrees that if it has or acquires hereafter any patent or interface copyright or other intellectual property interest dominating the Software, such dominating interest will not be used to undermine the effect of this Copyright Assignment. Open Source Project and the general public shall be and are licensed to use, in the Software, without royalty or limitation, the subject matter of the dominating interest. This license provision will be binding on the assignees of, or other successors to, the dominating interest, as well as on Contributor. This license grant shall be nonexclusive, royalty-free and non-cancelable.

7. Contributor is not obliged to defend Open Source Project against any spurious claim of adverse ownership, but will cooperate with Open Source Project in defending against any such claim.

8. Contributor warrants to Open Source Project that it is the sole copyright holder of the Software conveyed under this Copyright Assignment.

9. EXCEPT AS SPECIFIED IN PARAGRAPH 8, CONTRIBUTOR MAKES NO OTHER EXPRESS OR IMPLIED WARRANTY, INCLUDING WITHOUT LIMITATION, IN THIS DISCLAIMER OF WARRANTY, ANY WARRANTY OF MERCHANTABILITY OR FITNESS FOR A PARTICULAR PURPOSE.

10. This Copyright Assignment and all conveyances made pursuant hereto are deemed made in California, as of the date of fixation of any Software covered hereby in tangible form and, also, as of the date of execution of this Copyright Assignment by Contributor.

_____ Date: _____

Contributor

_____ Date: _____

Open Source Project

The GNU General Public License

Version 2, June 1991

```
Copyright (C) 1989, 1991 Free Software Foundation, Inc.
59 Temple Place—Suite 330, Boston, MA 02111-1307, USA

Everyone is permitted to copy and distribute verbatim copies
of this license document, but changing it is not allowed.
```

Preamble

The licenses for most software are designed to take away your freedom to share and change it. By contrast, the GNU General Public License is intended to guarantee your freedom to share and change free software— to make sure the software is free for all its users. This General Public License applies to most of the Free Software Foundation's software and to any other program whose authors commit to using it. (Some other Free Software Foundation software is covered by the GNU Library General Public License instead.) You can apply it to your programs, too.

When we speak of free software, we are referring to freedom, not price. Our General Public Licenses are designed to make sure that you have the freedom to distribute copies of free software (and charge for this service if you wish), that you receive source code or can get it if you want it, that you can change the software or use pieces of it in new free programs; and that you know you can do these things.

To protect your rights, we need to make restrictions that forbid anyone to deny you these rights or to ask you to surrender the rights. These restrictions translate to certain responsibilities for you if you distribute copies of the software, or if you modify it.

For example, if you distribute copies of such a program, whether gratis or for a fee, you must give the recipients all the rights that you have. You must make sure that they, too, receive or can get the source code. And you must show them these terms so they know their rights.

We protect your rights with two steps: (1) copyright the software, and (2) offer you this license which gives you legal permission to copy, distribute and/or modify the software.

Also, for each author's protection and ours, we want to make certain that everyone understands that there is no warranty for this free software. If the software is modified by someone else and passed on, we want its recipients to know that what they have is not the original, so that any problems introduced by others will not reflect on the original authors' reputations.

Finally, any free program is threatened constantly by software patents. We wish to avoid the danger that redistributors of a free program will individually obtain patent licenses, in effect making the program proprietary. To prevent this, we have made it clear that any patent must be licensed for everyone's free use or not licensed at all.

The precise terms and conditions for copying, distribution and modification follow.

Terms and Conditions for Copying, Distribution and Modification

0. This License applies to any program or other work which contains a notice placed by the copyright holder saying it may be distributed under the terms of this General Public License. The "Program", below, refers to any such program or work, and a "work based on the Program" means either the Program or any derivative work under copyright law: that is to say, a work containing the Program or a portion of it, either verbatim or with modifications and/or translated into another language. (Hereinafter, translation is included without limitation in the term "modification".) Each licensee is addressed as "you".

Activities other than copying, distribution and modification are not covered by this License; they are outside its scope. The act of running the Program is not restricted, and the output from the Program is covered only if its contents constitute a work based on the Program (independent of having been made by running the Program). Whether that is true depends on what the Program does.

1. You may copy and distribute verbatim copies of the Program's source code as you receive it, in any medium, provided that you conspicuously and appropriately publish on each copy an appropriate copyright notice and disclaimer of warranty; keep intact all the notices that refer to this License and to the absence of any warranty; and give any other recipients of the Program a copy of this License along with the Program.

   You may charge a fee for the physical act of transferring a copy, and you may at your option offer warranty protection in exchange for a fee.

2. You may modify your copy or copies of the Program or any portion of it, thus forming a work based on the Program, and copy and distribute such modifications or work under the terms of Section 1 above, provided that you also meet all of these conditions:

   a) You must cause the modified files to carry prominent notices stating that you changed the files and the date of any change.

   b) You must cause any work that you distribute or publish, that in whole or in part contains or is derived from the Program or any part thereof, to be licensed as a whole at no charge to all third parties under the terms of this License.

   c) If the modified program normally reads commands interactively when run, you must cause it, when started running for such interactive use in the most ordinary way, to print or display an announcement including an appropriate copyright notice and a notice that there is no warranty (or else, saying that you provide a warranty) and that users may redistribute the program under these conditions, and telling the user how to view a copy of this License. (Exception: if the Program itself is interactive but does not normally print such an announcement, your work based on the Program is not required to print an announcement.)

These requirements apply to the modified work as a whole. If identifiable sections of that work are not derived from the Program, and can be reasonably considered independent and separate works in themselves, then this License, and its terms, do not apply to those sections when you distribute them as separate works. But when you distribute the same sections as part of a whole which is a work based on the Program, the distribution of the whole must be on the terms of this License, whose permissions for other licensees extend to the entire whole, and thus to each and every part regardless of who wrote it.

Thus, it is not the intent of this section to claim rights or contest your rights to work written entirely by you; rather, the intent is to exercise the right to control the distribution of derivative or collective works based on the Program.

In addition, mere aggregation of another work not based on the Program with the Program (or with a work based on the Program) on a volume of a storage or distribution medium does not bring the other work under the scope of this License.

3. You may copy and distribute the Program (or a work based on it, under Section 2) in object code or executable form under the terms of Sections 1 and 2 above provided that you also do one of the following:

   a) Accompany it with the complete corresponding machine-readable source code, which must be distributed under the terms of Sections 1 and 2 above on a medium customarily used for software interchange; or,

   b) Accompany it with a written offer, valid for at least three years, to give any third party, for a charge no more than your cost of physically performing source distribution, a complete machine-readable copy of the corresponding source code, to be distributed under the terms of Sections 1 and 2 above on a medium customarily used for software interchange; or,

   c) Accompany it with the information you received as to the offer to distribute corresponding source code. (This alternative is allowed only for noncommercial distribution and only if you received the program in object code or executable form with such an offer, in accord with Subsection b above.)

The source code for a work means the preferred form of the work for making modifications to it. For an executable work, complete source code means all the source code for all modules it contains, plus any associated interface definition files, plus the scripts used to control compilation and installation of the executable. However, as a special exception, the source code distributed need not include anything that is normally distributed (in either source or binary form) with the major components (compiler, kernel, and so on) of the operating system on which the executable runs, unless that component itself accompanies the executable.

If distribution of executable or object code is made by offering access to copy from a designated place, then offering equivalent access to copy the source code from the same place counts as distribution of the source code, even though third parties are not compelled to copy the source along with the object code.

4. You may not copy, modify, sublicense, or distribute the Program except as expressly provided under this License. Any attempt otherwise to copy, modify, sublicense or distribute the Program is void, and will automatically terminate your rights under this License. However, parties who have received copies, or rights, from you under this License will not have their licenses terminated so long as such parties remain in full compliance.

5. You are not required to accept this License, since you have not signed it. However, nothing else grants you permission to modify or distribute the Program or its derivative works. These actions are prohibited by law if you do not accept this License. Therefore, by modifying or distributing the Program (or any work based on the Program), you indicate your acceptance of this License to do so, and all its terms and conditions for copying, distributing or modifying the Program or works based on it.

6. Each time you redistribute the Program (or any work based on the Program), the recipient automatically receives a license from the original licensor to copy, distribute or modify the Program subject to these terms and conditions. You may not impose any further restrictions on the recipients' exercise of the rights granted herein. You are not responsible for enforcing compliance by third parties to this License.

7. If, as a consequence of a court judgment or allegation of patent infringement or for any other reason (not limited to patent issues), conditions are imposed on you (whether by court order, agreement or otherwise) that contradict the conditions of this License, they do not excuse you from the conditions of this License. If you

cannot distribute so as to satisfy simultaneously your obligations under this License and any other pertinent obligations, then as a consequence you may not distribute the Program at all. For example, if a patent license would not permit royalty-free redistribution of the Program by all those who receive copies directly or indirectly through you, then the only way you could satisfy both it and this License would be to refrain entirely from distribution of the Program.

If any portion of this section is held invalid or unenforceable under any particular circumstance, the balance of the section is intended to apply and the section as a whole is intended to apply in other circumstances.

It is not the purpose of this section to induce you to infringe any patents or other property right claims or to contest validity of any such claims; this section has the sole purpose of protecting the integrity of the free software distribution system, which is implemented by public license practices. Many people have made generous contributions to the wide range of software distributed through that system in reliance on consistent application of that system; it is up to the author/donor to decide if he or she is willing to distribute software through any other system and a licensee cannot impose that choice.

This section is intended to make thoroughly clear what is believed to be a consequence of the rest of this License.

8. If the distribution and/or use of the Program is restricted in certain countries either by patents or by copyrighted interfaces, the original copyright holder who places the Program under this License may add an explicit geographical distribution limitation excluding those countries, so that distribution is permitted only in or among countries not thus excluded. In such case, this License incorporates the limitation as if written in the body of this License.

9. The Free Software Foundation may publish revised and/or new versions of the General Public License from time to time. Such new versions will be similar in spirit to the present version, but may differ in detail to address new problems or concerns.

Each version is given a distinguishing version number. If the Program specifies a version number of this License which applies to it and "any later version", you have the option of following the terms and conditions either of that version or of any later version published by the Free Software Foundation. If the Program does not specify a version number of this License, you may choose any version ever published by the Free Software Foundation.

10. If you wish to incorporate parts of the Program into other free programs whose distribution conditions are different, write to the author to ask for permission. For software which is copyrighted by the Free Software Foundation, write to the Free Software Foundation; we sometimes make exceptions for this. Our decision will be guided by the two goals of preserving the free status of all derivatives of our free software and of promoting the sharing and reuse of software generally.

NO WARRANTY

11. BECAUSE THE PROGRAM IS LICENSED FREE OF CHARGE, THERE IS NO WARRANTY FOR THE PROGRAM, TO THE EXTENT PERMITTED BY APPLICABLE LAW. EXCEPT WHEN OTHERWISE STATED IN WRITING THE COPYRIGHT HOLDERS AND/OR OTHER PARTIES PROVIDE THE PROGRAM "AS IS" WITHOUT WARRANTY OF ANY KIND, EITHER EXPRESSED OR IMPLIED, INCLUDING, BUT NOT LIMITED TO, THE IMPLIED WARRANTIES OF MERCHANTABILITY AND FITNESS FOR A PARTICULAR PURPOSE. THE ENTIRE RISK AS TO THE QUALITY AND PERFORMANCE OF THE PROGRAM IS WITH YOU. SHOULD THE PROGRAM PROVE DEFECTIVE, YOU ASSUME THE COST OF ALL NECESSARY SERVICING, REPAIR OR CORRECTION.

12. IN NO EVENT UNLESS REQUIRED BY APPLICABLE LAW OR AGREED TO IN WRITING WILL ANY COPYRIGHT HOLDER, OR ANY OTHER PARTY WHO MAY MODIFY AND/OR REDISTRIBUTE THE PROGRAM AS PERMITTED ABOVE, BE LIABLE TO YOU FOR DAMAGES, INCLUDING ANY GENERAL, SPECIAL, INCIDENTAL OR CONSEQUENTIAL DAMAGES ARISING OUT OF THE USE OR INABILITY TO USE THE PROGRAM (INCLUDING BUT NOT LIMITED TO LOSS OF DATA OR DATA BEING RENDERED INACCURATE OR LOSSES SUSTAINED BY YOU OR THIRD PARTIES OR A FAILURE OF THE PROGRAM TO OPERATE WITH ANY OTHER PROGRAMS), EVEN IF SUCH HOLDER OR OTHER PARTY HAS BEEN ADVISED OF THE POSSIBILITY OF SUCH DAMAGES.

Index